ROSES AND THORNS

Concepción Cabrera de Armida
(Conchita)

Roses and Thorns

Revised by Mary McCandless
(Sr. Dolores Icaza, RCSCJ)

Edited by Ron Leonardo

ST PAULS

To: Chase w/ fraternal love
Chepe MSpS

Library of Congress Cataloging-in-Publication Data

Conchita, 1862-1937.
    [Rosas y espinas. English]
    Roses and thorns / by Concepción Cabrera de Armida (Con-
chita)
        p. cm.
    ISBN 0-8189-1239-1
1. Mary, Blessed Virgin, Saint—Meditations. I. Title.

BT608.5.C6513 2006
232.91—dc22

                                2006021662

Produced and designed in the United States of America by the
Fathers and Brothers of the Society of St. Paul,
2187 Victory Boulevard, Staten Island, New York 10314-6603,
as part of their communications apostolate.

ISBN 0-8189-1239-1
ISBN 978-0-8189-1239-9

Printing Information:

Current Printing - first digit   1   2   3   4   5   6   7   8   9   10

Year of Current Printing - first year shown

2007   2008   2009   2010   2011   2012   2013   2014   2015

Dedication to Our Lady of Solitude

M Y BELOVED MOTHER! I cannot write unless it be with your sorrowful heart. I have no ink unless it be your tears. I dedicate this little book to your loving solitude. Give me, Mother, even one sigh from your heart that it may breathe upon it and give it life for the good of souls that grieve and for the glory of your almost unknown sufferings during those years of absence from Jesus which preceded your glorious Assumption.

You are the consolatrix of the afflicted because you drank from the bitterest chalice.

You are the admirable mother in sorrow, tender toward those who suffer because you knew what suffering is.

You are the queen of martyrs; therefore you understand the heart that weeps; therefore you cure the wounds of the soul; therefore you will teach all your children how to suffer, how to attain heaven through the cross, how to sanctify solitude through love.

Table of Contents

Preface

Roses and Thorns is a journey by means of which we come to live, in imitation of Mary and with her help, in sympathetic resonance with Jesus' sentiments. It consists of a re-reading of the gospel, lived from the inside out — that is, from the point of view of Christ's sentiments, from one heart to another, adopting the same attitude as that of Mary.

In *Roses and Thorns*, Christ is always the center of the meditation. From the Incarnation to the Ascension, the gospel scenes become contemporaneous, as if they were taking place today and as if they were being related by a mother (Jesus' mother and our own mother), who lived them intensely for love of us. It is she who now accompanies us, with "an active and maternal presence" (John Paul II, Encyclical Letter *Redemptoris Mater*, 1 and 24), so that we might make them an integral part of our lives.

Upon recalling the gospel scenes, related and lived by Jesus' mother, all the major aspects of the Lord's mystery appear: incarnate Word,

Redeemer, true God and true Man and our only Savior, who seeks to save all humanity with our collaboration. At the same time, and almost imperceptibly, all the graces unique to Mary, which were granted her for our benefit, also begin to appear: She is the Mother of God and our mother, ever a Virgin, the immaculate one, the intercessor or mediatrix, assumed into heaven.

The uniqueness of this book, *Roses and Thorns*, lies in its taking, as a point of departure, an event or biblical text (as the Word of God), re-read with her as Mary might have, imitating her contemplative attitude. Reference is also made to the Old Testament and to the experience of the saints.

The dynamics of each theme — there are thirty-three meditations — is summed up in the words "**rose**" and "**thorn**." Mary communicates her meditation and life experience of a gospel event (for example, the Annunciation): it is a "**rose**" which she gives to us from her Son, so that we might allow His word to penetrate into our hearts. But Mary also lived this gospel event as a "**thorn**," which is to say, like somebody who shares the same fate as Christ, like a "sword" (Lk 2:35). Mary's deep sorrow consisted in seeing that the Lord was neither known nor loved. Then, as she maternally offers us her "**rose**," she invites us to accompany her in her sorrow (her "**thorn**"). As a good mother, she teaches us how to suffer with love, and to transform our suffering into gift.

Mary's maternal tenderness for each believer (then and now) is apparent at every moment. The "**thorns**" or sorrows of the Blessed Mother are an expression of this tenderness. She invites us to receive the "**rose**" for our consolation and surrender, keeping the "**thorn**" for herself, so that we might discover her motherly love and might keep her company. Conchita has Mary say, "The sorrows were all for me, but the precious fruit derived from them — for you."

It is important for us to emphasize the "timeliness" of this theme. Seeing the milieu in which the believer lives (in Conchita's time or in our own, which is very like hers), one is invited to an authentic ecclesiastical renewal. This renewal is not only a necessity, it is also a possibility. We can and we must become holy. Conchita always leaves one with the sense of determination that it can be achieved and that it is possible. We are never caused anguish; rather, in the light of Mary's maternal heart, we strive to enter into Jesus' Heart: "Remain in my love" (Jn 15:9). Mary, according to Conchita, is not only the Mother of Mercy, but also the Mother of Holy Hope.

When one reads this book, one feels invited to live in union with Mary, so that, with her help and by her example, one might better grasp the love and sentiments of Christ. The relationship with Mary develops into a friendly one. Upon grasping man's ingratitude toward Christ, our Redeemer, throughout the ages, the reader is invited and stimulated to become holy and to be an apostle. To love Mary or to be devoted to her is the equivalent of collaborating with her in the salvation of souls, that is to cause all humanity to encounter, know and love Christ, the Redeemer. To be able to do this, the believer must "contract," according to the Conciliar expression, Mary's "maternal love" (*Lumen Gentium* 65).

Possibly the most unique aspect in this book is the sense of Mary's "solitude," from the point of the Ascension of our Lord until her own Assumption. This theme is of utmost timeliness in order to help us to understand the meaning of our painful experience of God, Who sometimes seems to be silent or as if He were absent. Only an authentic Marian spirituality will enable us to decipher, by means of a living faith, that it is in silence that God's Word (the Word made flesh) echoes; and that it is in "absence" that a new presence of that Emmanuel, God with us, becomes reality. The mystery of suffering, which all of us experience, is unveiled only by sharing Christ's life, as Mary did, in order to "fill up" in our own lives what is lacking in Christ's passion (Col 1:24).

Roses and Thorns will be a classic of Marian devotion, as "The true Devotion of the

Blessed Virgin" (of St. Louis Marie Grignion de Montfort) and "The Glories of Mary" (of St. Alphonsus Mary Liguori) already are. As far as Conchita's literary expressions, one must keep in mind the psychological, cultural and social conditions within the context of the period in which she lived, as might be the case with any other book of a prior era.

The reading of *Roses and Thorns* is a model to help us learn to meditate upon other biblical texts, in a harmonious blending of faith and revelation, in the attitude of leaning one's head upon Jesus' chest, like the beloved disciple (cf Jn 13: 23). This attitude of being in tune with "Jesus' sentiments" (Ph 2:5) and of intimacy with Mary, receiving her "into our home" in a communion of life (Jn 19:27), might well be the best disposition to live the present historic moment of the Church, in relation to the entire liturgical year. From the Incarnation and the Nativity up to and including the Paschal Mystery and the effusion of the Holy Spirit, "The Blessed Virgin Mary accompanies us on this journey... the radiant dawn and sure guide for our steps" (John Paul II, *Novo Millenio Inneunte*, 58).

Mons. Juan Esquerda Bifet
Professor at Urbaniana
Pontifical University, Rome, Italy

Introduction

DEVOTION TO OUR LADY in her solitude is almost non-existent. The idea generally held about her last years has little attraction. Very few appreciate and meditate on Mary in this time of great sorrow in which she purchased, with her martyrdom of solitude, the graces we receive today.

This little book aims to bring everyone to love Mary in her sorrowful memories which most lacerate the soul; in her memories of one whose absence is most heartbreaking; in those tears without witnesses — those which scald the cheeks and tear apart the intimate depths of the being.

For what Mary did was to live with her memories of Jesus; to suffer for the absence of Jesus; to weep much for her exile without Jesus.

And what sacred fruit did Mary obtain from this great martyrdom?

Greater union with God… more adherence to His will… greater eagerness for heaven.

Certainly Mary was a perfect creature; but she was raised at each stage of her life to a perfection almost without limit, until she reached the zenith in her solitude which followed the Ascension of her divine Son.

Let us contemplate the Immaculate Heart of Mary crowned with **Roses** which represent Jesus, "the flower of the field and the lily of the valley," whose memories surround her in every instant of her martyrdom of solitude. The **Roses** seem incompatible with the heart distressed by sorrow, but thus it was: that what appeared as **Roses** in the eyes of men had for the Holy Virgin cruel **Thorns** of memory which, after the Ascension, pierced her so sensitive heart. Mary was all patience, love and smiles to her children; always interior were those incomprehensible torments which only God could see and understand because their depth was deeper than all the seas.

Graces and consolations were **Roses** given to her children, but unspeakable sufferings, unbelievable sorrows, mortal griefs for her.

We shall place in this crown on the heart of Mary the queen of martyrs, our most beloved mother, thirty-three **Roses**, representing the final traces of her passage through this earth, and we shall make clear the good and all the graces which the sorrows of the most pure Virgin have brought to us. She was a mother, and thus she acted: she embraced great sacrifices intimately concealed, allowing her children to observe only the beautiful harmony pleasing to them.

Let us then meditate on the **Roses** and **Thorns**, imagining that the virginal lips have said, "Attend, and see if there is any sorrow like my sorrow.... They have heard my groaning and there is none to console me" (Lamentations 1: 12, 21).

O pure Virgin, in my littleness and poverty, I shall lift my voice, asking all hearts to console you, my beloved Mother, and to pause on the road of their pilgrimage at least long enough to say, "Thank you."

I shall display your wounded heart, but at the same time I pray with tears in my eyes that the sword of your remembered sorrows will shatter my own hard heart. You who wounded the very heart of God with the arrows of your love, pierce my heart so that I may feel your sorrows and my ingratitude. God forbid that, having suffered such a martyrdom as your solitude, you have no children to console you.

The Blessed Trinity

*M*Y SOUL IS GREATLY indebted to the Blessed Trinity, my child. I adore Him without ceasing and in these unending hours of solitude, my gratitude keeps on growing as I think of the inundation of His goodness toward me.

I would like you to look for a moment into the eternal abyss of His graces and favors, through the lens of my **Rose** for today, so that you may help me to bless Him and give Him infinite thanks.

In the divine mind of the Almighty, I excelled as the firstborn among the pure creatures. Since earth was conceived in the mind of the eternal Father, He has loved me. He gathered all purity, love, and tenderness, and with that He formed my heart.

When the Creator extended the blue veil of the heavens, when He put an end to the abyss, when He marked the ocean with the stretch of sand which would bind it, I was there. When He was forming beings, I was a fixed idea in God, accompanying Him in His marvelous works.

The Word, that splendid beauty of the Father, loved me from all eternity. As His mother I was destined to be at the Incarnation, as the throne of wisdom—that is to say, the same Word. I was in the divine plan before all ages.

The Holy Spirit also had me in His heart as His beloved spouse from all eternity, calling me "slender as the palm tree," "beautiful as the flower of the pomegranate tree," "chosen as the sun," "a lily among thorns," "the immaculate"— filling me with His most exquisite graces from the time of my Immaculate Conception.

It is thus that the Father created all things with me; the Son came to redeem the world through me; the Holy Spirit lavished many graces upon the Church and the entire world through the merits of Jesus Christ together with mine. It is in this way that I have been the blessed and necessary instrument of the will of God for the creation, regeneration and glorification of humanity.

Because of the lofty designs that the Holy Trinity had on this lowly creature, there would have been no incarnation, no redemption, nor even creation without me, my child.

Why, then, does it seem strange to men to see my admirable privileges? Why do men deny my singular virtues, if I was conceived from all eternity and destined to be not only co-redemptrix, but also—in a certain sense—to be creatrix because in time I would be the Mother of the eternal Word and foundress of the Church together with Jesus and the Holy Spirit?

I was certainly—as one may say—necessary to the Father in order to develop this plan, and to the Son to carry it out. Likewise I was necessary to the Holy Spirit, who through me came to the Apostles, illuminating, vivifying, and perfecting the Church, and nourishing by my martyrdom a new people, present and to come, at the foot of the cross. I am—as St. Bernard would say—the world of the Blessed Trinity, and for that reason I was conceived in the divine intelligence before any human being entered the world.

The divine Majesty determined to create me in order that I might be the light of a love most gentle, compassionate, and tender. That is why He prepared for me a heart pierced by thousands of **Thorns**, even though it was crowned with **Roses**, so that it would bend like the delicate stem toward the dust of human miseries to bring them aid. For that reason I will always attend to the afflictions and needs of my children, and even after my death, I will descend to this earth many times: at Pilar, in Mexico, at Lourdes, at Fatima, to comfort the Church and convert millions of souls to God.

In paradise the voices of the Most High resounded, saying that I would crush the head of the ancient serpent; and hell will continue to roar forever, my child, but I will always be immaculate on the face of the earth, as I am now in the sight of the Blessed Trinity.

I meditate on the prophecies, seeing the goodness of God, my Savior, Who has done marvelous things in me. "A star from Jacob shall advance, and a bud will rise from Israel, who will produce a beautiful flower, the Spirit of God shall rest upon him." O child, child of my soul, breathe in the divine scent of this flower which I give you this day, and caress it, remembering gratefully the Blessed Trinity, loving God with all your heart and soul, with all your strength. Let it penetrate your heart with that divine life, loving ceaselessly until the end of time.

RESPONSE

O Mary, queen of angels and men, I love you and I rejoice in the grandeur of my mother. I venerate the prophets who through the ages have directed their eyes of hope and love to Bethlehem, Nazareth, Jerusalem, Mount Tabor, and Calvary, and remained so entranced in seeing your future heights of virtue. For forty centuries you were the fixed idea of these holy souls, who passed their lives being reminded of your sorrows, your strength, and your solitude. They could not speak about the Messiah without disclosing your love and your purity.

St. Cyprian says, "I read and I imagine that Mary is a spiritual world in a great and admirable way, the firm ground being her profound humility; the vast ocean, her immense charity; the heavens, her sublime contemplation; the sun, her clear understanding of the divine; the moon, her beauty and purity; the stars, the splendor of her perfect sanctity; and the brightest stars, the wonders of her most exalted virtues."

I dare say, my dear Mother, that the atmosphere of that beautiful world—in which shine your earth, ocean, sun, moon, and stars—is formed by your sorrows, the almost unknown martyrdom which weighted your soul down with its solitude, so that with the torments of this absence and with a great longing for heaven, you bought the graces which would lead us to Him.

O my beloved Mother, I rejoice at your unnamed heights. I thank the Blessed Trinity with all my strength for the reflection of His perfection which He communicated to you and with a cry of joy I exclaim, "What a privilege to have a mother who is a queen, but most of all, a mother who knows what sorrow is." Amen.

I will say the Gloria (Trisage) praising with all the fervor of my soul the Most Holy Trinity, and offering myself with perfect abandonment to the divine will.

The Annunciation

*H*OW MUCH I REJOICE and how much I weep in this solitude, my child, as I recall the steps of my existence that I am going to retrace with you. Come near to me, rest your head upon my heart, and listen to the memories of very happy times reverberating there. Listen attentively.

God lives in an ecstasy of contemplation of His own Divinity; in this lively and fruitful ecstasy the divine Word is born; and this Word-made-flesh through love sprouted from my bosom through the work and grace of His Holy Spirit. That is the beautiful **Rose** that I dedicate to you today.

One day forever blessed, while I was deep in prayer, I saw my room suddenly brightened with resplendent rays of light. There stood the archangel Gabriel. Sweet harmonies filled my ears. I could not understand that astounding picture. When the archangel greeted me, saying, "Hail, full of grace," I was very disturbed. What was the cause of that? With all my soul, I felt the full strength of spiritual modesty. Instantly, I could see all the virtues that adorned me, so many precious gifts hidden in my heart that I didn't know were there.

Because I was predestined to be the Mother of God, the archangel bowed before me. I blushed crimson when I heard the words, "Blessed art thou among women." There was a battle between my modesty and the favors which the Lord wished to bestow on me.

My heart is still moved when I think of the graces with which God has enriched me without my deserving them. My maternity is a sovereign mystery of atonement, of the union of God with man; it is the turning point from which the destiny of the earth rotates.

I, a poor servant of the Almighty, being consulted by God? Why would He ask my consent to give me such a precious gift? Why should I be considered to participate in the resolution of the salvation of the universe and discuss it with an archangel from heaven? How confused and humbled I was!

With what lively colors would that room be ever represented in my mind; that fortunate place which listened to the secrets of eternal love—that humble little corner in which, without the world's knowing it, the world itself was renewed and made rich with a treasure: heaven! Even though I was unknown by all on this earth, the gaze of God Himself was fixed on me. Because this agreement was not with man, an angel spoke with me and from his lips I listened to the announcement of my divine motherhood.

O sovereign moment when, through an angel, the Holy Spirit enlightened my mind with a celestial radiance and made me understand how the Holy One would make of me His temple, His spouse, and His mother. Never had anyone heard of such a prodigy. Through my humility and my God-given purity, I was to be the mother of my Creator.

The Holy Spirit, with great fruitfulness, would descend upon me. By virtue of the Most High, I would be overshadowed. He who by essence is grace and sanctity would unite Himself to humanity in my womb.

I would lose myself like a drop of water in the ocean of the perfections of the divine Word, Who would communicate to me a thirst to humble myself further and to look for depths in which to hide my exalted virtues.

I will place before your eyes a few brief reflections so that you may get a glimpse of the great things God has done in me. It would not be wrong to say that God, from all eternity, could create a human being each instant more perfect than the one He created before it. If He started with the highest angel, where would the limit be? What heights would the last creature reach? All this incalculable perfection would still be infinitely distant from the sanctity of the divine Word, that Word which became flesh in my virginal womb.

Not even a million new creations would compare with this one in which the Word would become incarnate. He could have redeemed you by becoming an angel, but He preferred to come down and become like dust, that is to say, man.

I imagine that in heaven a great clamor could be heard and that for an instant the infinite light would be extinguished. The splendor of the Father, the clearness of the eternal light, the God of God, would deign to come down to this earth more rapidly than a breath. Leaving His jeweled throne and the harmony and splendor of His kingdom, He would come down to the most exalted angels, the seraphim, and there He would be adored with the ardor of an intense love. Before Him they would form an honor guard. The divine Word, moved by this, would look at each one and say, "I am not looking for you; I am looking for man."

He would hasten on and meet the cherubim, the high and brilliant intelligences, who adore Him, honored at His approach. But even though He gazed at them with pleasure, He would say, "It is not an angel that I wish to be: I am looking for man." In the same way He would stop at the thrones, dominions, virtues, powers, principalities, angels, and archangels—and to each He would respond in the same way: "I am looking for man, I am in love with man."

Passing through immeasurable distances, leaving behind the sun, the moon, and the pearly clouds, He arrived at Nazareth—and to me, an unworthy virgin. Penetrating my immaculate womb, like a ray of light in a crystal vase, He became flesh and took human life in the "hand-maid of the Lord."

"The divine Beauty, to make itself loved," said a saint at a later date, "should put itself into action and manifest itself directly, in person. The Sun of Justice ought to be elevated above the earth at the zenith of its splendor, moderating the brilliance of its rays with only a pure cloud to surround it. And that apparition was to be continuous, daily in the Eucharist, so that the earth, being heated again with its rays, would not return to ice after a final sunset.

"The uncreated Beauty put itself into action. This substantial Beauty manifested itself to man. The Sun of the Divinity had to cross the immense horizons of heaven, in order to illuminate the narrow horizon of earth with its all-encompassing light."

The Word of God became flesh, the divine Beauty united itself with human nature. Beauty uncreated and invisible took a human form, visible, and tangible. The divine Sun arose surrounded by a cloud to soften its rays. And this Beauty, this Loveliness, this Sun would be my son; the Word deigned to appear in the Incarnation clothed in the sacred humanity which He received from me.

Submerge your soul in these profound reflections. Take the **Rose** which says "Love"— and rejoice in the ineffable mystery which it represents. It is crimson and white. Accept it, my child, to adorn yourself with it, a **Rose** uprooted from my heart. It is a memento of your Virgin Mother; it is a token which insures heaven which I purchased for you. Carry it in your heart and think of me when you see it, as the joyful Mother of Jesus.

The **Thorn** which this **Rose** leaves in my heart is the ingratitude of many who will pass through the world without giving the least thought to the incomparable benefit of the Incarnation.

RESPONSE

Virgin mother of my life, this holy mystery of the Incarnation thrills me, and my impoverished soul, breathing in its divine perfume, rejoices to imagine it with many vivid colors.

It overwhelms me, this contemplation of the infinite love of the Word. In His incomparable humility, He came down to your womb to be "the true Light which enlightens every man who comes into the world.... The Father sent Him through the Holy Spirit, and through you, so that He may sing a song of blessedness to us.… He placed His trust in Jesus so that we would love Him totally in relation to our humanity—His perfection of its harmony, wisdom, and attraction" (Tertullian).

My Mother, teach me, as your child, to be actuated by this love, and to return thanks with all my soul for the overwhelming favor, well-known but inexpressible, which elevated our nature to heaven. If God did not seek to be happy without man, neither do I, Mother, desire any other happiness than He. Amen.

I will offer an act of humility by doing what is most difficult for me to do.

MEDITATION III

"*Fiat*"

*F*IAT! MAY IT BE DONE!" This word was a living **Rose** for the world, and particularly for you.

The archangel had completed his heavenly message. I was overwhelmed by the glory of the grace. I had only one question in order to preserve my vow of virginity, and that was: "How can this be done?"

The reply satisfied my concern for chastity—I learned that "the Holy Spirit would come upon me, the power of the Most High would overshadow me, and therefore the Holy One to be born of me would be called the Son of God."

The archangel did not go away; he awaited my freely-given consent in a respectful attitude—and so... I considered... this alternative was given to me: either your liberty or your captivity; but I, comprehending my future sorrows and faintly surmising something of Calvary, in order to save you, I remembered that the archangel had told me that the Kingdom of God would have no end; and I saw you there, my child, across the ages falling into hell if I refused my consent.

What did I feel at that time?

My soul thrilled with a most ardent love; my heart burned with gratitude. Crossing my hands upon my breast, lowering my eyes trembling with holy joy, I exclaimed, "Behold the handmaid of the Lord. Be it done unto me according to thy word."

At that happy moment, the Word was made flesh and you were saved by your adorable Redeemer, because Jesus is the bond that binds the world to God.

My faith in the words of the sovereign God, Who is eternal truth, was great. I believed simply, and without a shadow of doubt, what was proposed to me. "Do not fear," said the archangel, and I did not fear; I believed that I could become a mother without ceasing to be a virgin because the very Author of my virginity, to Whom I had consecrated my body and soul, would know how to guard them. O marvels of the secret of God, which still deeply moved me, I remember today in my tremendous solitude.

That day passed; Jesus came to my arms; He died on the cross; He rose from the dead, He ascended into heaven—and all because of the *fiat* which made the world shudder with happiness.

What would you have done without this word that released a torrent of bitterness for me, and one of infinite mercy for you? Heaven was closed to you by sin, and then this single word from my lips saved the universe. God decided that this mystery should depend on my consent—voluntary, free, and spontaneous. Oh, this sensitivity of God astonishes me!

The world waited four thousand years for the arrival of the "handmaid of the Lord" because He would not violate the freedom of the human soul. He respects this liberty because He is God.

That day was a joy for the angels; ruin for demons; and the salvation of sinners. The divine plan was realized through my virginity, my humility, and my faith.

The promises of God were brought to

fulfillment: the vows of the patriarchs, the sighs of the just, the groan of men and their cries of impatience asking heaven to drop down its dew, that earth might bud forth a Savior.

All this was for your happiness, but I knew very well all the **Thorns** which it contained for me. I was to be the mother of the Victim of your salvation. The Word, not being able to suffer and die in His divinity, determined rather to take a body from my body, and blood from my blood, in order to sacrifice them for you; He comes even now as your daily nourishment. I had compassion for you; and since that instant I offered myself as victim with the Victim, in the same spirit of sacrifice and desire for your good.

Now, after the drama of Calvary, I have lived years and years in a martyrdom of solitude, in a certain way completing payment for your salvation, your sanctification, and the degrees of your glory in heaven. There still reverberates an eternal *fiat* until there is no longer a grace to be purchased for my beloved children.

Child of my sorrows, take this **Rose**, pure as light, which my heart, full of tenderness, gives you today. You will find the word *fiat*, written on its petals, so that you remember all the days of your life, and especially today, the great love your mother holds for you.

I admire your humility, beloved Mother, in the midst of your grandeur. I venerate your loving sacrifice, your accepting all future sorrows so fearlessly and freely. I appreciate your compassion and affection for me, and take pleasure, my Mother, in the delicate attentions of your incomparably loving heart.

Just as you were a virgin because of your purity, you were a mother only through your humility; without this humility the Holy Spirit would not have descended into your immaculate womb. What would I have done then? I congratulate you, Mary, and I pray that your virtue be infused into me so that I obtain what is lacking in my proud heart: humility.

O so greatly beloved handmaid of the Lord! Let me learn to humble myself and always submit to God's will because I desire to imitate the self-effacement of my mother, to be nothing, to disappear, to flee all worldly honors, and hide from the gaze of men, always trying to imitate her solitude.

Thank you, my Mother, thank you! Emotion steals my voice, and kneeling before you, I bless and admire the divine instant of your loving *fiat* which is remembered three times a day, enthusiastically welcoming the sound of the Angelus and the thought of you. Happy am I to have so loving a mother.

Today I will repeat the short prayer,
"Behold the handmaid of the Lord," doing
the will of others rather than my own,
unless it opposes my conscience.

Jesus

WHAT MORE LIVELY and delicate **Rose** can I give you today than the sweet name of Jesus? It was I who conferred this blessed name on Him because the archangel said to me, "You shall conceive and bear a Son, whom you shall call Jesus." What a beautiful name, my child! Jesus, which means Savior; a name which you ought to carry always in your heart and in your soul; which will be both the first and the last name on so many lips; which so many millions of martyrs will write with their blood; which so many of the just will engrave upon their hearts.

This blessed name came from heaven to soothe you and give you rest. And for how many blasphemies will that sweet name make reparation! How many agonies it will soften! How many sorrows will it relieve!

My ears were chosen to hear that adorable name for the first time, and its fate was revealed to me. I weep now, in my solitude, with gratitude, always with gratitude, recalling these favors from heaven.

On countless occasions your lips will invoke the name of Jesus, hardly giving a thought that the name making you so happy came into the world through my conduct.

Is it not true that the soul, on pronouncing it, feels the same sensation as at receiving a caress? The adorable name resounds in heaven, on earth, and even in hell, the name at which all knees bend; this holy name should also be your breath and your strength.

Therefore, this is the **Rose** which I take from my heart to perfume your life, to brighten your path, to carry to your lips, and to impress deeply in your loving soul; this shall crown your brow in heaven.

A delicate **Rose** for my children, the name that your lips should pronounce, enjoying its infinite sweetness.

But what else was it for me? A flower with **Thorns**, and that because considering that Jesus means Savior, I saw in my soul nothing less than the death of my son being made a Victim. My heart would be handed over to the most cruel suffering, that I had to sacrifice Him and even see Him die in order that men might live.

The eternal Father asked this because He so loved the world that He gave it His own Son; and it was His will that I should also love the world to the point of giving the world that son of mine, the Son of the Most High and of the handmaid of the Lord.

Yet how beautiful He was! "Beautiful in His form," says the prophet. "The grain of the elect" and "the wine that brings forth virgins," says another, referring to the Eucharist.

And in his preface to Psalm 44, speaking of the beauty of the incarnate Word, St. Augustine would say: "The Word was wedded to the flesh, and the bridal chamber was the womb of the Virgin." But Who is this Who descends to be wed? Listen!

"'In the beginning was the Word, and the Word was God, and the Word was with God.' Beautiful as God, and when He was alone, established in God; beautiful in the womb of the Virgin when, without losing His Divinity, He took on humanity; beautiful newly born as an infant; beautiful in heaven and on earth; beautiful in the womb of Mary; beautiful in His miracles; beautiful in His scourging; beautiful inviting us to life; beautiful despising death; beautiful leaving His holy soul in the tomb and taking it up again; beautiful on the tree of the cross; beautiful in the rock of the tomb; and eternally beautiful in the heights of heaven."

And the divine Beauty before my eyes shed the last drop of His Blood nailed to the cross. This sorrow was so deep and immense as to embitter every beat of your Mother's heart. Looking at Him, I saw the Redemption, and I felt all the swords that were to pierce my heart each time that I lovingly called Him. This blessed name, which my lips conferred upon Him the first time that I held Him in my arms, this name, which was solemnly given to Him at the circumcision, was my delight and my torment, my sweetness and my agony. Your **Rose** and my **Thorn.**

RESPONSE

O Jesus! Jesus of Mary, and also my Jesus! That name so enchanting and divine, that falls from heaven for my happiness. You are the sweetest melody in my heart, light in my sorrows, strength in my battles, fire in my tepidity. Priceless **Rose** of Mary! You perfume my life in such a way that all the charms of earth disappear for me. You are the supreme ideal of all beauty. A child can contemplate You without fear; the faithful heart places happiness and confidence in You. Oh, would that my poor soul could think of nothing else than uniting with You!

You are Jesus, my Jesus, throne of all grandeur, resplendence, sublimity, and tenderness. How can we not love You with all our hearts? How can we not lose all to find You? How can we not ignore everything else because of knowing

You? How can we not abandon all to seek You?

O Mary! His adorable name never leaves me without hope and it makes my soul long for heaven. Thank you, my Mother, thank you. Mary, you are blessed a thousand times for giving me a Savior! When will I know Jesus to Whom I owe so much? From the depths of my soul I long to possess Him day and night.

I love Him, my Mother, more than my own soul. I love Him because He is your heartbeat and my life. I am anxiously longing to go to your side to contemplate Him. Is it true that, when I go to heaven, you will tell me, in that intimacy, all of His excellence? Shall I see Him in every way and in every age, always full of love for this child of yours?

O my sweet Jesus, while I journey in this exile, give me an ardent love for You which will totally consume me. Do not conceal Yourself from me, my good Jesus, and let the fire that burns in me be such that it may set my heart constantly on fire with endless longing to con-template You. Let my dying lips pronounce Jesus, Jesus, Jesus. And let me die in order to live with You and with Mary for all eternity. Amen.

I will repeat frequently with my lips and with my heart: "Jesus and Mary, I love you with all my heart." I will prove my love with deeds, returning good for ill, smiling patiently.

The Visitation

*M*Y CHILD, I never attempted to scrutinize God's plans concerning me; I always submitted to His will and desire. Humble and confident, I abandoned myself constantly to the divine will, following the inspiration of the One Who was director of my soul: the Holy Spirit. I owe Him so much, my child; I love Him so much; I have so deep and indissoluble a unity with the third divine person that He is like the soul of my soul.

He is my consolation and my strength, and even more so since that unforgettable day, Pentecost. Since that time He is my heavenly delight and the source of my peace. Love Him especially as "Father of the poor," and the light of your heart. It was He Who disclosed the mystery of my divine motherhood to my cousin, Elizabeth.

"Mary arose and hastened over the mountains," says the evangelist. I was moved by a divine inspiration, because calm and gentleness were the center of my life. I was moved by the Holy Spirit, Who blew me there. Nobody on earth knew my secret; nobody saw that light, that fire which was leading me and which came to illuminate and embrace the world.

But, scarcely did Elizabeth hear me when,

inspired by the divine breath of the Spirit, she exclaimed in a loud voice that still echoes in all hearts and here in mine: "Blessed art thou among women and blessed is the fruit of thy womb." The archangel had already spoken those words, to my confusion, but at the same time the Holy Spirit repeated them through Elizabeth's lips, adding, "and blessed is the fruit of thy womb. And whence is it that the mother of my Lord should visit me?" asked Elizabeth. Even St. John felt the approach of the Lamb Who takes away the sins of the world.

"Oh, blessed art thou who has believed"—continued Elizabeth (that is to say "I was His mother because of my faith")—"because the things that were said to you concerning the Lord shall be accomplished."

And I—so discovered—what did I do? I burst into a canticle of love. My soul filled with holy thoughts, overflowed, glorifying the Lord because He had looked graciously upon His handmaid. O child of my soul! My tears flow at the memory of those happy days in which "the Lord did great things for me," and marvelous wonders.

Do you see the consequence of following this inspiration—to what this act of love leads and how God rewards it, making it radiate good to many? "All generations shall call me blessed," my child. And with extraordinary power I felt "what great things the Almighty was pleased to accomplish in His poor servant, the handmaid of the Lord." I do not know how I, your mother, who had no sentiment except humility, assumed such impulses toward grandeur, those accents of glory in order to praise the Omnipotent. Truly I was in an ecstasy of humility; and the sight of my lowliness and the feelings of the greatness that belonged to God were like magnetic poles that met in my heart.

Those great things were crystallized in my divine motherhood, and for this reason "all generations shall call me blessed." And thus the echo of the divine fruit of this august mystery comes to you.

Here I am, after once again recalling the most glorious and the most sorrowful events of my life, enduring the **Thorns** of these memories without my Jesus, removed from the One Who is my life in this valley of tears. But I remained on earth in order to dry your tears and to form, petal by petal, the flowers that crown my heart. Each petal is a martyrdom, which is why it holds the fragrance of heaven.

Each **Rose** is a mystery of wisdom, of virtue, and of a conquest of graces, prepared for you with the sorrows of your mother, who lives only in these memories, whom your good alone sustains, and whose only consolation is the desire to show you that she is your mother.

O heavenly and blessed Mother, pleasing, amiable, and loving, always serving others and forgetting yourself! You have never had a heart to deny any service, and always help with your gaze fixed upon God.

Who could have witnessed this scene and that sublime debasement of your soul without being filled with emotions of deep gratitude?

Never did the inspiration break forth with more plenitude than in this marvelous canticle; to which many ears in the world have not yet become accustomed even after twenty centuries. You, Mother, held the knowledge and feeling of your greatness in your heart, and nevertheless, called yourself the "handmaid" of the Lord.

From whence did you receive those divine accents? From whom those sentiments of your own lowliness that shone in the depths of your humility? Thinking that the world would honor God in you, you accepted the profound submission of St. Elizabeth, summoning the coming generations to celebrate you. Although unknown to all the earth, you foresaw that all generations of humanity would call you blessed, and so the prophecy was fulfilled. There cannot exist a single Christian heart that does not acclaim you blessed, who does not admire your divine motherhood, who does not find joy in your singular excellence.

Mary, you are glorified in all languages, because while you were aware of the highest possible graces, you concealed this marvel in the obscure humility of a hidden and austere life.

I praise you, and with you, my soul magnifies the Lord. I admire you as the star of first magnitude in the Church, and I rejoice to see you reign in the world and in every heart.

I love you, my Mother, and I ask you through the sorrows of the solitude in which you remembered these marvels, to teach me the true humility that does not consist of disregarding the favors of heaven, but in attributing them to God, penetrated with our nothingness and profound misery. Amen.

Today I will visit a hospital or some sick person, in honor of Mary, speaking of her with much fervor and causing as many hearts as I can to love her.

MEDITATION VI

Bethlehem

*I*N BETHLEHEM I give you the bud of a heavenly **Rose**. Behold it in my heart—so pure, so white, so fresh and fragrant. See how happy, tender, and perfect it is, bedewed with tears of my

Child, Jesus. You will see how much I thought of you at this time, presenting this **Rose** of my immaculate heart to you.

Jesus came to save you, to teach you all the virtues which He Himself first practiced; He came to buy heaven for you with His Blood—to die for you on a cross so that He may be with you always.

Look at His glorious little eyes which already seek to gaze at you; see those rosy lips, which already utter your name in order to declare His love for you; see His little hands of ermine which are eager to bless you. Behold Him thinking of you, crying for you, asking that I, His humble mother take Him to your side and place Him in your arms to caress you.

This tender Child who weeps is the Almighty, Who seeks to touch your heart. This Child, Who cannot speak yet, is infinite activity which nothing wearies; this Child is the Creator of the universe, eternal Wisdom, supreme Beatitude. This Child will be a martyr of love for God and men, Who will sweat blood, Who will die on a gibbet; He is everlasting Beauty, Life itself, limitless Glory Who will give Himself to you as food in this world.

Jesus is incarnate beauty. Why did He become man? Why has He taken the appearance of an infant in all of its weaknesses? Why would He impose labors, humiliations, and even a cruel and sorrowful death upon Himself? Why indeed, my child? Only to conquer your soul, only to unite Himself to you in a most intimate manner, and to raise you to heaven, because He could not suffer His heart to live apart from you.

Why should you not love Him? Why should you not adore and serve and sacrifice yourself in His honor?

Is it not true that this divine Jesus is the best and most wonderful **Rose** that the heart of a mother could offer you today? Do you accept it, child of my soul? Yes, of course, because you are the chosen child of my tenderness.

O sorrowful remembrance of the attentiveness of my Jesus! When I think, here in my solitude, of the tenderness with which His infinite love honored me, I cannot explain the sublime experience of my grateful heart. Cardinal Berulle says that it was my privilege and blessing that my son wanted the world to see Him as a child, in a state in which I was joined to Him.

Jesus desired to depend on my care and my service, as familiar and intimate as they are sacred for a mother. He wished to receive the first adoration in the manger from me, as well as the last in the Eucharist today.

How would I have borne my solitude without Him? He surrendered Himself to me without reserve, the very Son of God, in order to give me His first smiles, in order to let me dry His first tears, set flowing even in His childhood by the ingratitude of men. All the graces of His heavenly infancy delighted me.

How can I not weep with gratitude at the remembrance of all these things, which are stored in my heart to relate to you now, far away from the world, ever since the terrible drama of Calvary where He declared me your mother?

In Bethlehem my soul was pierced seeing the King of kings in a cave of animals. My heart ached with foreboding, knowing that men of the time expected the Messiah; and later, through the word of the Magi, knew the time of His appearance in the world, yet no one ran in search of Him, nor wished to place Him on a throne to pay Him homage; but rather, my child, they sought only to kill Him. Such was man and so he will always be.

This was my **Thorn**. But your fragrant **Rose**, I repeat, will be He Who came down from heaven for your salvation. It will be Jesus, Who eagerly desired to give you a heart that would beat like yours, Jesus Who would come to smile on you, to give you favors, to hide you in the depths of His heart.

Come, draw near to me, so that you may be first among those invited after many centuries to meditate with me on these **Roses** and **Thorns,** in the martyrdom of solitude and comfort, of glory and blessings for your soul.

My Mother, already sorrowful in the cave of Bethlehem—O holy Virgin, who begins and continues life in me by your martyrdom! I have not thought until now of that epoch of your life of solitude, of the many years which, after the death of the one solace of your existence, your divine Jesus, you spent watering the valley of misery with your hidden tears.

I was ignorant that your sorrows, caused by human ingratitude, would purchase for me, in union with the merits of Jesus, every single grace that I have received and that soothes my pains. I feel happy to come each day for the **Rose** which is taken from the heart of my loving mother and which perfumes my steps upon the earth with the aroma of the virtues it bears with it.

My Mother, pardon my past ingratitude; and since you have considered me worthy to receive the **Roses** of your heart in the life of Jesus, I run with all my soul to see them, in order to refresh myself with their beauty; and to guard them as in a sacred reliquary in my soul which is all yours.

But, O holy Virgin, I am your child! and since I enjoy these flowers, I also desire to weep with you for the cruel **Thorns** that your love would spare me, for the hidden martyrdom in which the stars of your virtues shine. I also desire that my heart be pierced and that I weep as you have wept, to console you.

On seeing you as charming as you were at Bethlehem, I wish to think that you are the same as the one I shall contemplate later, splattered with Blood on Calvary, and to accompany you as a true child, most loving and grateful to such a good mother. Amen.

I will give alms to the poor children
of some institution.

MEDITATION VII

The Presentation

AFTER ALL THE HONORS and praises of the archangel, of Elizabeth, of the Magi, and of the shepherds, I wished my grandeur to be diminished by the Purification, a humiliation to which all women submitted. I was blessed; Jesus, the fruit of my womb, was blessed; and thus I was not obligated to this act. But, although elevated by my privileges, I hid the height of my divine motherhood and my virginity from the eyes of the world; I stripped myself of this double glory for the sake of humility, for resemblance to my Child Jesus, who humbled Himself even to becoming man for your love.

I was the first altar on which the heavenly

Victim descended, attracted and summoned by my love; and I was the first priest to offer this Victim to the eternal Father in the Temple of Jerusalem for the sake of the world. I lifted in my arms, and raised to heaven, that pure and immaculate Host which would be consumed on the cross. I offered the Redeemer of the world thinking that this action would be renewed in each one of the masses that all priests should celebrate, always in union with me. I had in mind the ministry that those priests ought to carry out: a ministry of purity, of sanctity, of transformation through imitating me.

Therefore I have so great and intimate a part in the Mass that all priests ought to invoke me and be accompanied by me in order to celebrate fruitfully.

Oh, if they did, my child, what holy priests there would be! How I would remind them that they should be like angels! How I would make the divine Word known to them, the Word that would inspire them in knowledge and heroic virtue. Sacrificed by me at the foot of the altar solely for your salvation, the Redeemer of the world is offered in remission for your sins. That trait of sublime detachment was my **Thorn,** my child, to hand over my treasure to the death by which you would find life.

Furthermore, there was a **Thorn** for me in the words of Simeon, which embittered my soul for life; sorrow without a name, hearing that Jesus was destined as the ruin and resurrection of many in Israel, and to be a sign of contradiction. And certainly, how many doubts in my children! Even now there are those who speak like the Jews, "How long are you going to hold our souls in suspense? If you are the Christ, tell us openly." Their pride blinds them, child of my heart. "I am speaking to you, and you do not believe Me. The works that I do in my Father's name give testimony of Me." But "The light came into the world, and men loved the darkness more than the light, for their works were evil; he whose works are evil abhors the light, and will not go where his works can be reprimanded." So responded Jesus.

But the world will be shattered at the triumph of my divine Son. Nevertheless, I am a mother, and I am grieved at the loss of many souls without faith, blind and obstinate in their errors. Do not be one of those, but be in the number of the saved, since Jesus also came "for the resurrection of many," and only those who voluntarily reject grace will perish.

Simeon said, "This child is destined for the ruin and the resurrection of many in Israel, and as a sign of contradiction." Then he continued immediately, prophesying, "And a sword shall pierce your own soul." What sword? To see my children wander down the slope of vice, scorning the Gospel.

Stay and see if there is a greater sorrow for a mother than the eternal misfortune of her children. Today, therefore, come repentant to the deep wound in my soul, which desires to guard you there, to cherish and defend you against your enemies.

I am your mother, your loving mother, and I want to hide you as the apple of my eye, to conceal you with my mantle, to shelter you in my womb, to withdraw your eyes from the sight of evil and your ears from all false doctrine that would plunge you into hell.

Follow the road of humility and of faith; sacrifice your own judgment, believing in Jesus, and place all your confidence in me. Then you will never be lost, for such a humble one is saved, and the humble one is my true child who lives in the shelter of my goodness and love. I come to offer you as a victim in my arms, like Jesus, and this will be your **Rose** for today. What happiness for you if He accepts you as atonement for such great crimes!

RESPONSE

Astonished by the humility that you show in the mystery of the Presentation, I draw near to you with my **Rose** in my hand, begging that virtue which is so necessary if my proud spirit is to become an acceptable victim. You, Mother, would have fled, escaping all praise if you had been capable of thinking that you deserved it. You always long to hide the virtues which adorn you, to anonymously live the common life.

You preferred to suffer a cruel martyrdom by concealing even from your virginal spouse, St. Joseph, your dignity as the Mother of God; you preferred to appear with the blemish of all mothers rather than exempt yourself from what did not concern you, since you were immaculate. Give me your prudence, Mary, your love for the hidden life, without ever seeking to shine in this world. Give me a lively faith that I may confide, without faltering, in the divine will.

Mary, in honor of your co-redeeming humility, I ask a special favor today, that you lend me this precious Child that I, too, may offer Him in my arms as an oblation to the eternal Father in expiation for all my sins and as an act of thanksgiving for all His blessings. Grant me this, Mother, so that after I have been pardoned by the merits of this precious offering, I may close my eyes to the world and all its vanities, and open them only to holy things; until the day comes to contemplate you in the infinite heart of God.

I will not speak of myself; I will avoid flattering the vanity of others, and when I hear others praise me, afterwards refer it to God, remaining happy in my nothingness, in imitation of Mary.

The Flight into Egypt

MY CHILD, "Jesus came to His own and His own received Him not." He came to give life, and some, even from His early childhood, sought to give Him death. With what sorrow I recall the night of terror in which an angel told my spouse Joseph that we must flee into Egypt with the Child because Herod sought to kill Him.

You ask the question: "Does a God flee from a man?" My child, when a valiant soldier runs from combat, it is tactically rather than fearfully; these were contrived attacks of that supreme action which could only be consummated on the cross. But my mother's heart trembled; at the same time, it adored the sacred designs of this Child in His state of flight, who was already the terror of the kings whom He came to destroy, and the joy of the humble on whom He came to bestow His graces.

It was not Herod who obliged the Son of God to flee, but the Son of God who wished to do this. He did not flee out of fear, but by design; not out of need, but of power. There He was to seek out sorrow for the continuance of His path to Calvary in a burning desert, through a pagan land, by suffering the hardships of the long road in bad weather, by living in even greater poverty, exiled and without liberty, hiding Himself from men for your salvation.

The angel could have told us to flee to the home of our relatives, but no, Jesus wished to be alone with me in a foreign land in order to have only me, with no other throne but my virginal lap, no other caress but that of His mother, "the handmaid of the Lord" and that of my loving spouse, St. Joseph. How can I not recall this delicacy of the heart of my Jesus, that moves me to the depths of my being?

My soul was crushed by the pain of what He was to suffer, not because of my fatigue and inconvenience; He charmed me with His beauty, absorbed me in those mysteries which I meditated in my heart. The deep wound that had been cut into my soul by the prophecy of Simeon kept throbbing by degrees with the presentiment of the future, but then my thoughts of you and of how our pain would affect you in future centuries consoled me. This was one drop of honey in the midst of great bitterness.

The echo of the wailing mothers whose children were sacrificed to save the life of the Savior—those innocent flowers, the first of the martyrs—reached me; my soul was drowned in sorrow, and I hugged that Treasure in my arms against my heart. What caresses of filial love, those of my Child, Jesus! He clung to my neck, and I wished to return Him to the shelter of my womb, because already I saw Him as "a sign of contradiction."

It was in Egypt, along the green banks of the Nile, that my divine Child pronounced His first word: "Mother" and there took His first steps in the wilderness that was later colonized by the hermits. Here the angels surrounded Him lovingly, gathering to serve Him; but He, Whose delight was to be with the sons of men, wanted only my hand to serve Him, my arms to rock Him, my songs to lull Him.

Let me weep recalling those enchanting scenes, which made me happy in the midst of many privations. How easy it is to suffer with Him. How sad, how difficult to suffer without Him!

Take your **Rose** which holds the picture of Jesus in my arms, pointing to my heart. Look carefully as He says to you, "Come to her," and do not pierce my heart with a **Thorn** by loving the danger of sin and perishing in it.

Flee, my child, from your enemies. Here you have the Holy Family that loves you, that offers you a hiding place, that gives you a humble shelter, that desires the gift of peace and holy joy for you at the side of the Child Jesus.

RESPONSE

Yes, my Mother, Yes. I agree to live retired from the world and its vainglory in the blessed company of this Holy Family. What peace! What happiness! What a sweet and comforting joy my soul experiences at the side of these who care so much for my soul. How I shall learn, in silence, work, and abnegation, to take rest for myself only in Jesus.

I will help you, Mother of my soul, with your precious burden. I will work to nourish Him in the poor, and in the Church. I will lose myself in the contemplation of His virtues. O enviable exile with Jesus! O delightful days that will rapidly pass listening to the beating of His heart. This is the life of a saint: to model oneself on the life of immolation that Jesus led.

I ask to unite myself with the Child Jesus, becoming a child for love of Him. I want to allow myself to be guided by His example, to suffer pain serenely, and to see you in all things—you, my beloved Mother. I cannot imagine without weeping from loving admiration, His first divine steps, His divine dreams, His love for suffering.

O Mary! Make me as a child because children are not condemned. Children are the preference of Jesus, Who says with His own divine lips that of such is the Kingdom of heaven. Amen.

I will dress a poor child, aiding his mother
in honor of the martyrdom of Mary.

The Lost Child

*T*HERE WAS a fresh blow to my loving heart; in fact, my child, life was a series of blows that martyred my innocent heart. One sorrow was followed by another and another, as an introduction to other greater ones which awaited me: the cross, the absence of my son, the solitude in which I live.

Well then, returning from the Temple of Jerusalem where we had gone to fulfill the Passover law, we lost Jesus. How frightful was the grief of St. Joseph and myself! For three days and three nights of anguish we looked for Him along roads and villages; but no one gave us any news of the Beloved of my heart.

What my heart endured at that time no one can conceive. Can you even imagine Mary without her Jesus, the Virgin Mother without her divine son, the immaculate sheep without her holy Lamb who takes away the sins of the world?

Finally, after three deathly days for my heart, we found Him in the Temple among the doctors who looked upon Him, overwhelmed with His wisdom. Wonder flooded our hearts; we had found the Heaven of our home Who, increasing in age and wisdom among men, was already "employed in the things that concern the service of the heavenly Father." He was the Light which illumines all men who come into the world and shone in the darkness which did not comprehend it.

His loving heart was so powerfully moved that, at the sight of my tears, He came to hide Himself in Nazareth, close to me, until the age of thirty. O my son, O Jesus, my Jesus! How can the humility of the handmaid of the Lord repay You Your loving kindness, obedience, fidelity and subjection to me?

Oh, what a fragrant **Rose** is my gift today, my child, bought with the **Thorn** of three days of indescribable torment. Receive it with my counsel—which will serve you well in absence from Jesus.

Look child, when He is lost to you: search in the temple. I mean not so much in the Church, though He is there. I wish to speak about the interior of your soul, the temple of the Holy Spirit. Take care that in your temple external things do not cause a disturbance, and the darkness of deliberate faults do not rob you of the vision of your Loved One. Seek Him always, for Jesus takes joy in being sought, because this grief proves your love to Him. He finds so little love in hearts, even in those who call themselves His own. And He yearns to be sought... and found!

How many souls are lost in the spiritual life,

and lost because they will not use their talents, will not be moved, will not sacrifice in search of Him. He suffers innumerable disappointments with many hearts that become lukewarm and insensitive and do not awaken.

I humbled myself although I had no fault. Night and day I wept and sacrificed myself until I found Him. You must do the same. Do not tarry, do not live without Him Who is your life. Do not let up in your exercise of piety: do not let your heart become dejected, but let it be more ardently inflamed with love for the absent Beloved One. And then, if after having done this you do not find Him, think that you are glorifying God by this sacrifice and suffer in peace, exercising faith, hope, and charity with an unselfish and pure love.

Always believe in the promise of Jesus, hope in His word which does not pass away, and love Him, love Him very much, with all the strength of your soul and in whatever state of spirit, only for being Who He is, abandoning yourself to His will.

Pray with urgency to your loving Father, my child; tell Him to give Jesus to you because He is yours, all yours. Invoke the help of the Holy Spirit. Think of me, think of me, smallest child of my soul, and suffer the divine dispositions in peace; and if your will is the will of God, He will know, in His generosity, how to reward you. Rest in Jesus, who although you do not see Him or feel Him, never abandons what is His. Kiss His blessed hand, which wounds you, with adoration, with respect, with veneration.

How beautiful it is, when dealing with God, when the soul wishes to manifest its fidelity in desolation, absence, and desertion. Happy is the soul that practices that holy complacency in God, when its love does not find Him. This generosity of the pure heart charms Jesus and inclines Him to give Himself to that soul, to console that heart, to transfigure that life which knows how to love even in the dark hours of faith.

Within your **Rose** of today, my child, find this advice and much affection from the loving heart of your mother.

RESPONSE

Thank you, Mother of my life, thank you for this holy advice that teaches me to carry, as I ought, the cross of the perceived absence of my God. I promise you that I will follow Him, seeking Him without rest, until I have found Him. For is it not true that love penetrates all darkness, tears aside all veils, overcomes all obstacles, and reaches the heart of Jesus?

Is it not true that tears move Him, and generosity in sorrow attracts Him? Is it not true, Mary, that having recourse to you with a pure heart, the Jesus Who was hidden returns to our arms? Is it not true that He listens to a lively faith and firm perseverance, and that the Holy Spirit never denies Him to simple hearts which see Him not only for themselves but moreover for others?

O my Mother, it is also certain that when absence is prolonged, the soul, overcome with sorrow, weeps at a loneliness which seems interminable. Then what better time to accompany you in your martyrdom, to run to the Sanctuary with you, and there, with obscure faith, place the grievances and complaints of love in your heart, and **give** instead of **receiving**?

At last the day will return; at last dawn will bring the light; at last the cold will cease with the fire of the divine Sun: Jesus Who was lost only to give us the joy of finding Him again.

Nothing shall be too much for me to suffer for love of Mary. Suffering or relief, consolation or discouragement, life or death—I shall joyfully accept all of these in order to please her.

He Was Mine

HE WAS MINE. For thirty years, Jesus belonged to me. Do you understand that, my child? Can you by any chance measure the capacity of my heart to contain the wealth of confidences, of intimacies, of holy conversations and secrets which Jesus had with His Mother? If in three years He completely filled the world with His most blessed words, what would He not share with me in all that time?

But I kept all those things in my heart, and only in the "Magnificat" did I permit myself, with sublime enthusiasm, to let go of that which overflowed from my heart. Oh, marvelous silence, which wrapped me in obscurity! Humility without a name! Discretion which I observed in order to speak to your soul in my solitude!

Well, yes, my child; Jesus communicated His plans of redemption to me, which caused me extreme sorrow. He spoke to me of the **Roses** for you and the **Thorns** for me, and my heart trembled before future scenes of blood, of martyrdom, of death on a cross for Him Whom I most loved. The hours passed with His divine head in my lap as my Jesus spoke to me of the Eucharist, of His indispensable humiliations, to cure your pride; of His vehement desires to be baptized with "a baptism of blood." I saw Him dreaming of the cross and awakening full of joy upon catching a glimpse of it. He confided to me how He came to establish the law of love, the law of charity, to love enemies; to pardon oppressors; to preach the Gospel to the poor, presenting them with the Kingdom of heaven.

He would preach new doctrine, which came from the heart of God for the transformation of the world; He longed for the moment of sacrifice to prove His love with sorrow, with immolation, with sacrifice.

My most loving Jesus conveyed to me what He loved: purity and the pure of heart; the treasures which are hidden in tears, in sorrows, in the cross; and how He came to give the knowledge of the heavenly riches of suffering, and the sweet fruits of suffering with Him.

O my child! The cross captivated Him and I trembled, certainly not on account of my own suffering, but because of having to see Him suffer and die in burning love for men, many of whom would scorn Him.

He came to make people love to do what the world abhors, to transform the universe, immersed in sensuality, to take away its horror of suffering and say, "I am with you in your tribulation." "Come to Me all you who labor and are burdened and I will refresh you"; to teach that love removes all weight from the cross; that suffering borne through His love is the pearl of eternal life; that the soul will feel His sweet yoke when it carries pain with resignation and generosity.

And I listened with eagerness to those exalted lessons that illuminated my mind and moved my heart with the abundance of His infinite mercy.

What days, what delightful hours we spent—at the side of Joseph, my spouse, listening entranced to the mysteries of love which fired our hearts with the same flame that burned in the heart of my Jesus.

I foresaw the fruit of this celestial doctrine which would transport you to heaven, and the most fragrant **Rose** of your love for the cross, with my **Thorn** and my thistle covering it so that it would not wither up while you contemplated this delight. To Him I said, "For this soul, my Jesus, I desire a special love of the cross; for the soul that is going to suffer greatly, I desire a **Rose** to lighten its sorrows." And thus, at that time I purchased it for you, and then I carried it in my heart so that today you could draw near to take it, and to weep over its precious chalice for your unfaithfulness.

RESPONSE

Mother of my soul, I would give a thousand lives to hear the divine confidences which the loving Jesus placed in your virginal heart. How rapidly those hours must have passed in which your heart, skipping a beat, was absorbed into the heart of your Jesus-Victim.

What would He tell you, Mother, thinking of me? That I would be ungrateful, unfaithful to Him Who loved me so much; how cowardly I would be in carrying my cross and following in His footsteps; how my inconstancy would wound Him; how my uncharitable acts would sadden Him; how my pride and my haughtiness would be like thorns in His adorable heart; but that He desired me to be pure, patient and self-sacrificing, not being satisfied with saving only my soul, but that I would bring many others to His feet so that they might know, serve, and adore Him.

O Mother of my soul! What have I done to please Him? What is there in my past life except seeking myself and forgetting Him? How many are my sins! What wasted graces have left His designs incomplete for me! But today, holy Virgin, I beg that you obtain pardon for me, telling Him that I am going to be good, lead an interior life, and meditate every day on the **Roses** and **Thorns** of your heart.

Let your sorrow be a comfort for so many souls like me, who have lived culpably apart from your lessons; let me approach you so that I can, at your side, hear the divine voice which invites me to be crucified with Him, to learn to love Him in the sacrifices which please Him, and to say in His ear that I also desire Him to be all mine.

Today I will guard silence for the space
of half an hour, repeating from time to time
with much love: "You are mine and
I am all yours!"

Saint Joseph

MY CHILD, would I have had the heart to leave you without the special **Rose** of my love, that which bears the perfume of the holy chastity and sweetness of my spouse Joseph? Never! I desire today to make a swift sketch of the virtues that I so admired and contemplated during the long years that I lived in his company.

His obedience had no limits. It was enough for him to receive divine communication in simple dreams to believe them—because his humility was so great that he did not believe himself deserving of being favored with brilliant revelations from heaven. His simplicity was perfect in every respect.

Jesus was his delight, his life, his reason for being; and it was he who had the joy to be chosen from among all mortals to serve as the representative of the eternal Father who abundantly communicated to him his sublime love of fatherhood for Jesus. He was also chosen to conceal my virginity and my divine motherhood. He hid this beautiful mystery until God wished to manifest it to the world. Jesus always passed as his son until that day of His Baptism, and later, on Mount Tabor, when the world listened, trembling, to that heavenly statement of the eternal Father: "This is My beloved Son in Whom I am well-pleased."

Almost all the saints, my child, had a mission to preach Jesus Christ, to proclaim Him shouting, to carry His light and His blessed name, even to the ends of the earth. But Joseph, says one author, is a saint unique in every point, predestined for a ministry entirely contrary: the mission of hiding His glory, of softening His reflection, of fostering His delay.

And Jesus loved him so much that He refused to give him the pain of seeing Him die by crucifixion. He was carried off before that, laden with virtues and merits, to the bosom of Abraham, from there to join the blessed in heaven.

My child, how much we loved him, Jesus and I! Joseph was the trustee of my secrets. His was a soul most holy among all the other saints. Together we endured the poverty of Bethlehem, the travel in the desert, the deprivation in Egypt and the joy in Nazareth. Together we looked for Jesus in the Temple when He was lost, and wept together in holy jubilation. His hands labored to feed us, and our company—Jesus' and mine—relieved all his hardships. How many times he carried the Child in his weary arms, and was comforted with His heavenly caresses! Later Jesus helped him in his tasks and labored to earn bread. But he suffered an interior martyrdom which shortened his life, and which he hid in order not to afflict us.

Joseph had a vague glimpse of the passion of Jesus, of my nameless suffering, of my present solitude without his companionship to console me, and this torment led him to weep in silence.

I who could read his angelic heart saw all this suffering, which so afflicted him. At times my respect kept me silent; at other times I comforted him with my words, helped him by uniting my grief with his, and communicated the confidences of Jesus which would sweeten his bitterness.

I had the happiness of serving him, of obeying him, of being his solace. I assisted him at his death, more holy and happy than that of any other mortal. In the arms of Jesus and with me by his side, he died as though falling into heavenly slumber.

Saint Joseph is the model of fathers, of

husbands, and of the interior life. Love him, my child, and make him much loved. If you seek to please me, you cannot do anything that makes me happier than to have a filial devotion to him, to give him honor in your home, and to imitate his virtues. Take him as the patron of your interior and spiritual life, and you will advance greatly towards perfection.

The spiritual fruit of my sorrow at his death whom I loved so much will be a **Rose** for you; and I will take charge that, with his radiant hands of glory, he will present you, at your death, with all the **Roses** of my heart which you have received, in the eternal mansion of the just, where unchangeable joy is firmly and truly established.

Oh, you who feel the deep need for loving and being loved! You who need an affection that never betrays you, a union that even death cannot break! Come to place yourself under the protection of my chaste spouse, in order that even on earth you may begin to live the heavenly life, that divine life of union with Jesus, because you know that life without Jesus is no life at all.

RESPONSE

O glorious St. Joseph, more holy than all the saints! How I rejoice to invoke you and remember the privileges with which the eternal Father distinguished you above all other mortals.

He determined that Jesus be called "your son" with all the sweet rights of a father, and Mary "your wife." What happiness also is yours, what power to help them with material aid and loving solicitude; what joy in keeping their lives protected and tranquil. I congratulate you, most holy Patriarch, for those delightful hours you spent joyfully contemplating Jesus and happily enjoying the beautiful interior and exterior beauty of Mary. Constantly you studied them, drawing sweetness, patience, and self-denial from their hearts.

I envy you, blessed St. Joseph, for no one knew as you did the secrets of Jesus and Mary, their zeal, the heroism of their sacrifices, their immaculate purity and the martyrdom of love in which their lives were consumed.

How beautiful and simple did you see this innocent dove! And how greatly you suffered at the vision of her martyrdom without you, the solitude of the wife whom you loved so well. Oh what martyrdom wracked your soul at the forevision of the passion and the seven swords which would pierce the Immaculate Heart of Mary. You dreamed of her alone, alone without Jesus—and this affliction embittered your happy life. And although I am worth nothing, I come to comfort and console you today, to say I will never leave her. But grant me the grace, as much as possible, to make myself less unworthy of her confidence, to bring to her feet many children who will love her in her final solitude and her martyrdom of absence. Amen.

Today I will distribute some pictures and medals of St. Joseph to extend his devotion, remembering the love he had for Mary.

Cana of Galilee

THE COROLLA of your **Rose** for today says "Mercy" in letters of gold. And in truth, what other thing could come forth from the fountain and ocean of mercy except mercy, says St. Bernard. For what reason does the vase guard the perfume if not to conserve its pleasant scent? Jesus filled my soul to retain all the virtues in it.

What perfect harmony between the heart of Jesus and mine! Because of that similarity of compassion and mercy, I one day said to Jesus: "They have no wine." I knew that He could turn stones into bread and would later change wine into His Blood, that there could be a miracle of goodness resulting from my request. I knew His heart so well! I was not ignorant that the hour for His miracles had not yet come, but I did not hesitate to believe that He would give His mother the favor she asked for. I had absolute confidence in Him, and the key to His loving Heart was mine.

I said only four words to Jesus: "They have no wine." I advised the servants then, "Do whatever He tells you." But Jesus, anticipating the path of His miracles, the splendor of which offended His humility, to give me joy, changed water into wine in the sight of all. "And His disciples believed in Him," says the evangelist.

There Jesus began the working of His miracles through my intercession: the torrent of spiritual graces with which He would change the souls of sinners into saints. My child, here you are feeling my maternal influence, and so, can you doubt that I am the omnipotent supplicant, in my character as mediatrix, and as your mother?

How moved I am when I recall that day of immense gratitude for my maternal heart! This is your **Rose**; but Satan does not persist in anything so much as in snatching the souls of sinners from me so that they do not cease to hear temptations and sink in the current of their vices; this is my **Thorn**, for am I not a Mother?

If you seek me in earnest, teach those souls what my heart is like; how it is presented full of **Roses** to attract them; how my heart says "Mercy"; and how no one has come to me in vain.

Friends abandon you, my child, but I,

never. In peril call on me, lift your eyes, see the star which beams on you. I am the mother of beautiful Love, and brilliant light from my heart shines for those devoted to me.

O my child! Never leave my embrace. The cross is the road to heaven, but I shall lighten the cross, I shall lessen this pain, and I shall be the strength and comfort of those souls who place their confidence in me. I will never abandon you; surrender yourself today to my motherly arms, and your heart and soul will be filled with consolation.

In each of my children I see a brother or sister of Jesus; and that vision suffices for me to sow joy in their path. "One only is your Father and that one is in heaven," said Jesus. "Go, tell My brothers that I go before them into Galilee where they shall see Me," He said to the holy women.

Be certain, child, that Jesus is your brother by His Father and mother. When you pray, pray as He said one day to His disciples, "Our Father who art in heaven." And on the cross, looking upon me with infinite love, He said, "Woman, behold your son." How then should I not love you if you are the brother of Him Who is so beloved; if your father is the Father of Jesus and His mother is yours? Here is the ideal of brotherhood and motherhood. You are in the family of Nazareth in which dwelt hearts that were treasures of love. So you must not fear.

Think that this will make you happy, and that we are prepared to defend you against enemies. But before you leave me today, receive some counsel from your loving mother.

Live from now on as if you were to die tomorrow; cast from your heart the love of earthly things to think of paradise; give an abundance of alms, and break with all that seems vanity and pride; do not humanize what is holy, this costs much; purify yourself from all that is not God, or which is not for His love; lift your heart from all human considerations to celestial things: your life ought to be divine, removed from this earth which could stain it. And earth stains so easily, my child.

Take flight from this world and live, like St. Paul, with heavenly thoughts and desires. Drop worldly and social demands, as often as they are occasions of sin and place your soul in danger. Make your life divine in God, I repeat, supernaturalize your actions, keep your heart pure, and I assure you of a reward in glory without end at our side.

O most loving and beloved Mother! Through whom, if not through you, has appeared in the world, under the form of humankind, the goodness of God, our Savior, Who is the resurrection and the life?

What a brother you gave me in Jesus! What a sweet gift you bring! What a fountain of love! And if He came down from heaven through you, it was to show me that I should also ascend to Him through you, following the advice you have given me.

Tell Jesus what I need, holy Virgin, so that I may acquire what I lack to resemble this family! And how great it is! You see that I am not humble, not patient, not mortified; that I look for my self-interest in things large and small, and live clinging to earth with my heart full of degrading inclinations.

Tell Him that when I draw near the wedding of the Lamb in Communion, I lack love, the beautiful wine of charity. O my beloved Mother, obtain this for me from our Jesus. Grant me this favor, most holy Mother, so that those around me may believe in Him as at Cana, seeing my vices changed into virtues. Amen.

Today I will give some altar wine to a poor church in honor of Mary.

Encounters

*F*IVE PRINCIPAL encounters with Jesus oc-
curred during my life, five meetings which
I tenderly recall today.

In Bethlehem, recovering from that ecstasy
of love, I saw Him for the first time, when an
angel, kneeling in an attitude of adoration, offered Him for me to take in my arms. O happy
night! This encounter filled me with a burst of
joy, and tears of tenderness. It was an encounter
of love—with my Savior, my son, my all.

I held Him in my arms, I offered Him
to His divine Father, I warmed Him with my
fragrant breath. On my lap I placed Him—He
who sustained the universe; With my milk I fed
Him—He who created me. In swaddling clothes
I dressed Him—He who clothed the world with
light and flowers; and I laid Him in a manger—
because I knew that He would redeem pride and
pleasure by poverty and pain.

But this stable should be, when you come,
a school of sanctity; in it the Eucharist is born,
the sweet food of the soul. My heart weeps as I
recall this incident in my life, the first encounter
of my eyes with the eyes of my son, of my most
loving heart with His.

This is your **Rose-bud**, to open in the

warmth of my love; this is my **Thorn,** to nourish Him for death on the cross.

My second encounter was in the Temple, after having lost Him, after existing without warmth, without light, without life. It resembles only those years of my solitude without Him. This was a new blow to my loving heart; the trial, the greatest sorrow, perhaps, equaled only by my unparalleled jubilee upon encountering Him at His post, admired by the doctors for His divine wisdom.

Then I pressed Him against my breaking heart and we went together to our beloved Nazareth so that we would not be separated for many years: how rapidly they passed by, leaving indelible traces on my heart! I nourished this white **Rose** for you, in order that He might be crucified.

O child of my soul, the third encounter was in the street of Bitterness where I saw Him bleeding; He was a single great wound, panting, with a cross on His back.

Upon seeing me silent, my eyes reddened with tears, He stopped, smiled, and wiping the blood which covered His divine eyes, He gave me a look of sorrow and of love. From His eyes, I absorbed the magnitude of His sorrows. How accustomed I was to understanding Him! My heart was breaking because there was no outlet for my overwhelming maternal love and sorrow. A mob of people surrounded me, but I saw only Him. Oh, such oceans of pain! Oh, what a flood of anguish! Overwhelmed, without strength, with the weight of the cross. I saw Him fall, collapse, strike the earth two or three times with His most holy face—the God of heaven and earth! I ran to raise Him; I wished to embrace Him, console Him, and kiss Him. He was my son! But I was brutally rebuffed.

Then I saw how, with horrible blasphemies, the executioners beat Him with their hands and feet so that He would follow them with the cross in the direction of Calvary. It was for your salvation, to open the locked door of heaven for you. This is your **Rose** with my piercing **Thorn.**

The fourth encounter was at the Resurrection. O joyful and beautiful encounter! My soul arose with Him, and in an instant my heart passed from death to life. Jesus came to me, radiant with beauty, glorious and resplendent, flooding His humble mother with jubilation. To console me, He wanted me to taste the divine balm of His presence. What more could I desire? My agony was changed into a flash of glory. It was He—my Jesus, my son, my companion in sorrow—triumphant over death. O fortunate moment! I kissed His side, radiant with light, and His feet, and I felt an indescribable joy, the blessedness of heaven on earth.

What a brilliant **Rose** for you, evidence of

His Divinity! But my **Thorn**, what was it, then? It was that I must let Him go again, that my heart must be nailed in that martyrdom of my solitude, that of His absence renewing my sorrows.

And the last encounter on earth? Which was it? Can't you guess? The Eucharist which is my life in this exile, that which calms my longing for heaven; He, my Son, He in the Sacrament, He the daily food, the strength of my soul, the life which sustains me, which makes me a martyr by the desire to contemplate Him, face to face in the bottomless depths of infinite perfection, in the ineffable ecstasy of the Blessed Trinity.

In my body, I am a prisoner on earth, but my soul, which lives within the sanctuary, mounts again to higher regions, submerged in the immense sea of the Divinity.

Your **Rose**, here, is the martyrdom with which I buy heaven for you, and my **Thorn**, Oh, "to die because I cannot die."

RESPONSE

I desire it, holy Mother of my heart; I desire it with all the strength of my soul: to encounter Jesus. And it is so easy to encounter Him for one who loves Him... but look, my Mother, at each stop I encounter myself with my arrogance and murmuring, with my vanity which is very much alive, with my dissipation and little correspondence to grace. I am a sewer of sins and miseries; I live very far from mortification and virtue, in isolation and emptiness of soul, but I desire to encounter Jesus. Lead me by the hand to where He is, whether it be Calvary or heaven. Here, every day I will look for Him in the tabernacle and say to Him, "Lord, behold, he whom You love is ill," or "Lord if You will, heal me," or "Lord, I live entirely alone, but I desire to find You. I am blind, give me light to see."

I desire to live before You like the lamp in the Sanctuary. Oh, if my blood could be the oil which feeds its light! But no, the lamp is the star of the Magi which only guides me to You there, but in receiving Holy Communion, I encounter You. Oh, yes, You will be mine so that we will never be separated.

Will you give me this, pure Virgin? Yes, you will give me this, and each day of my life I shall receive Him from your pure hands, and in my last Communion as a viaticum, when His heart beats within me, Gate of Heaven, lead me to Him, and give me that delightful encounter to cast myself into His embrace. Amen.

In honor of the most holy Virgin,
I will seek out a person against whom I hold
some resentment, and be kind, doing some
good toward that person.

Mother!

*Y*OUR **ROSE** of today holds a most beautiful title, sweet and delicate to your heart; it is "Mother."

"The power of the Most High shall overshadow you, and for this reason the Holy One to be born of you shall be called the Son of God," the angel had said to me, and I was a mother... and of what a son! Just as He made Himself responsible for the satisfaction of sin, so He became love for the mother, tender and pure, of that Son most beautiful and most loving.

I was the Virgin mother, mother of the supreme Love. I loved God in my son and my son in God. How profound! My love for Jesus was the most delicate, strong, and sacred, the most marvelous of all loves. And my love for you, child of my heart, was derived from that of Jesus. Mother above all mothers, I gave you life at the foot of the cross, and this I continue giving you in my solitude, preparing you for heaven.

"Do not forget the sorrows of your mother," says Ecclesiasticus, and I say the same to you today from my solitude on earth. Remember what you owe me and what I have been for you, and you will not sin.

In the sound of my voice you will hear that

of my Jesus, as the Apostles did who held His memory in me. In the brightness of my eyes you will see reflected the Beloved of your soul, and in the contact with my heart you will feel the quickened beats of His, who suffered so much for you.

If you wish to know Jesus, here I am. My appearance is the same as His, externally and internally. So much did I resemble Him! And how could it be otherwise, since I lived with His life, since I was an echo of His sentiments, since my soul vibrated with the same sounds of sacrifice which were in His soul?

He would not leave you an orphan; therefore, I am here these years of exile, preparing your patrimony in the Church, your heritage in the same Body and Blood which nourished me; and I pass the hours as the first worshipper of such a great Sacrament, thinking of you, praying for you.

Do not fear, my child, for you have a Mother, a solicitous Mother, always ready to dry your tears. I am the Mother of Holy Hope. Revive then your faith and never stop from placing yourself under my care. Pray to me in your difficulties, for I am the Mother of Good Counsel, and I can give you eternal life. Do you believe, perhaps, that I do not understand you? Remove that negative idea from your mind, because every mother always understands her children, even though they cannot speak to her.

Look; you offend my Jesus because you do not think of me; you feel the pain of solitude because you do not seek my company; you weep, my child, because you do not confide in my heart which always beats for you. When, orphaned and alone, you follow the path of vice, when trying to forget that I am your mother and you sink into your abjection, I shall weep for your ingratitude; but, at the same time, I shall fly to overtake you, to gain your good with my caresses and my pardon, with my **Roses** and my sacrifices, to wipe the sweat from your forehead in your agony, to wash you with the precious Blood of my son, and I will receive you into my heart, presenting you to Jesus, covered with my tears, in order to gain heaven for you.

Do not fear, child, for I am your mother. You have a mother and are blessed. In this **Rose** which today is plucked from my heart, see the word that is written: MOTHER. Look at it when enemies surround you, when your power falters and temptations envelop you, when the tempests of passion overcome you, and remember that you are not alone, but with me, always ready to console you, to save you, to run after you in order to rescue you from a fall into the terrible fires of hell. I love you so much! You cost me so much.

My Mother! Allow me to weep upon your lap for my disloyalty and ingratitude. I have run in pursuit of pleasures, snatched at by worldly things; in arrogance, I fled from you, Mary, who, as a shining star, appeared in the darkness of my conscience. I am ashamed to think that I call upon you only during necessity, and not to console you or think of you in your sorrows. If I suffer, it is because I have sinned. But you, Mother, you suffer only to gain pardon for me. How can I repay you for such a deep love?

My faith wavering, sad and wretched most of the time, I scarcely called upon your name with my guilty lips. But you were in the depths of my heart, Mother, and my sins were not powerful enough either to erase your memory or to blot your beloved image from my soul. And that was, without doubt, because you were praying for me, and because, although my works do not identify me as your child, always, always you are my Mother: you extend your arms to me, you come out to meet me, you show me your blue mantle filled with stars; you weep for my sorrows and wanderings, you lull me to sleep and watch for my waking, always smiling like the dawn, showing me only the **Roses** of your heart.

Here I am then, my Mother, repentant and humble. Neither creatures nor even the blessings of God were enough for me, and I sinned. Let now the teaching of the redemption and of the martyrdom of your solitude suffice to make me holy. If I do not lose God, if I do not lose you, my Virgin, what does it matter if I lose the whole world? I see myself forgotten by many. But you will not forget me! Punish me, according to your wisdom, with the tenderness and mercy of your motherhood. Tell your Jesus that now I am really going to be good, and I will never sadden your heart, the only heart that calls me "child." Amen.

> Today I will give a gift or dress to some poor mother, and I will do something for the good of her soul.

You Are My Son!

LISTEN, MY CHILD. I received the prelude to the Sacraments in the Incarnation. Because the Eucharist is an extension of the Incarnation: the divine Word in human form, giving His flesh to be consumed, becomes, in a certain way, our flesh, in an extremely close union.

The Incarnation was the first Eucharist, the first Communion of the world with God; and I was the first one to receive the Bread descended from heaven in order to give it to you. I gave my flesh to the divine Word to feed you, and the heart of a man, in order that He might love you with it. I myself was, to Jesus and with Jesus, the substance of this Sacrament as He was the substance of my life.

See how I love you, my child, who has given you my very blood in Jesus. "Christ, having taken His flesh from the flesh of Mary," says St. Augustine, "is the flesh of Mary given us to eat for our salvation." See whether I am truly your mother!

Jesus instituted the Sacrament of the Eucharist, saying, "This is My Body; this is My Blood." And before twenty-four hours had passed, with the same lips He pronounced, "Behold your mother"; and it was because He not only gave Himself to you in order to nourish you as your food, but also to give me to you as your mother.

Can you find a **Rose** more fragrant and of greater value than this one that I give you, with its petals formed from my own substance and life? How can you not love it, my child, if it is the greatest gift that He could give you; if it is your heaven on earth, your fortress, and in it, the One Who prays, sighs, and wishes to pardon you. There I have all the riches of His divine Heart for you. And what does He ask in exchange? A remembrance—only a remembrance—of Him and me in His Body and Blood. Will you refuse this? No, I know you. You are weak, inconstant, disloyal; but you love us much. Isn't that true? Would you truly not give your life to defend this Sacrament, to confess your faith, to extend the reign of Jesus in the Eucharist?

All those blessings of the Eucharist are the **Rose**, which I rejoice in offering you and which crowns my heart so that you may approach and breathe its pure fragrance.

But look, my child; your grace pierces my heart and I think, in my solitude, of the millions of sacrileges, of the horrible ingratitude of men who do not know how to appreciate this immense gift. I weep—and weep much!—for the blasphemies against this Sacrament of love; I weep for the abandonment given Him in the sanctuaries during this century and other centuries. I weep for the insults, the horrific hatred of which He will be the object, this Jesus, so good, generous and patient, Who came into the world in order to shed the rays of paradise upon your soul! My heart anguishes, thinking of the souls who will pass through the world without saying, "I love You!" I groan and redouble my love to pay for their coldness and failure to love Him who is Love itself.

This is my life now: to make up for ingratitude and to purchase grace for you with the suffering of my remembered sorrows. But, what? Will you now leave me alone in this life of reparation? Is it possible, my child, that, nourishing me with my flesh in that of Jesus, that, my blood running through my veins in those of Jesus, you would not kneel daily before the altar and adore the Sacred Host, you would not remove the **Thorns** from His sorrowful heart by loving the sacred tabernacle? Oh, no! You will come on your knees to repent, attracting many adoring souls who will repent for the sins of the world and acquire graces by prayer, mortification, and love, united always with me in my bitter sorrows.

You will come with a pure soul to drink at this fountain of Blood which brings forth virgins, because your body is not only a temple, but a chalice destined to contain the Body and Blood of my divine son.

Because of this you will be pure, the reflection of your immaculate Mother; you will fly with the strength of your zeal to ignite hearts with the ardor of charity, to extend devotion to the Holy Spirit, the beginning and end of all perfection; you will take the thorns from the adorable heart of Jesus, and, fastening them in your own heart, serve as balm to His wounds.

Will you promise all of this to me today, my child?

O holiest Mother, dry your tears, for I promise what you ask. But grant me what I am going to ask you in order to be able to give you joy. I believe, but fortify my faith; I hope, but strengthen my hope; I love, but increase my love; my sins weigh upon me, but stir up my repentance; I desire to weep for your sorrows, but make these echo in the heart of your child. Direct me, Mother; guide, lead, and protect me. I offer you in your solitude, my intelligence to think of you, my words to speak of you; my works and my labors to be suffered for you. I desire what you desire, Mary, but enlighten my understanding, set my will afire, purify my body and sanctify my poor soul that my pride will not entangle me, nor praise alter me, nor the world deceive me, nor Satan seize me.

Purify my memory, holy Virgin, restrain my language, recollect my vision, correct my evil inclinations, cultivate my virtues, and above all, my Mother, cast into my freezing heart one spark of the fire of your charity, so that it will thaw my heart to tenderness for your sorrows. Amen.

I will choose suffering with an ardent
desire for purification. I wish to detach
myself in total renunciation and in complete
sacrifice, to be more like Mary.

Resurrections

*M*Y CHILD, you can rise to the life of grace if you believe in God, if you love Him with all your heart.

One day, the leader of the synagogue, Jairus, was with Jesus, asking Him to go and cure his daughter, when messengers arrived to tell him that his daughter was already dead. But Jesus said to him, "Do not fear. Only believe and she will live." And thus it was. Everyone laughed, knowing that the girl was indeed dead, but Jesus said to them, "Move out of the way; the girl is not dead, but asleep."

Then He entered the house with her father and mother, and taking the girl by the hand, He said, "Child, arise," and the girl once again began to breathe, and at that point she got up and began to walk. And Jesus told them to get her something to eat.

Jesus wanted you to know that, when you have fallen into venial sin, you are sleeping and are not listening carefully to the inspiration of the Holy Spirit; it is necessary to rise from tepidity, to take His hand, my child, and above all, to receive Holy Communion. Oh yes, to eat the most holy Body in order to regain strength to once again follow the way of the cross.

In the beginning of the spiritual life there are many souls who, like the daughter of Jairus, sleep, and they even appear dead to the touch of grace; they fall and there they lie; and it is beneficial that other souls have recourse to Jesus in their favor.

But you my child; if you fall, lift yourself immediately and do not allow any mortal sin, which is its death, to enter your soul.

But another day, on entering the city of Naim, Jesus came upon a funeral procession. The one who had died was the only son of a widow, and the poor mother was walking behind the body. Moved to the depths of His heart, thinking of me (who had lost my husband, Joseph, and would soon be left without Him), He said to the mother of the young man, "Do not weep." Jesus cannot see tears without being moved; and especially a mother's tears: those He keeps in His heart.

He never closes His heart to the sobs of a mother. And why? Because of me, my child, whom He loves so much.

Opening a passageway, Jesus approached, touched the bier, stopping those who were carrying it, and said, "Young man, I command you, arise!" The dead man sat up and began to speak, and Jesus gave him to his mother.

A tender passage which so touched the delicate heart of Jesus! Does it not move you even to the depths of your soul? See, little child, when souls are dead to the life of grace through their sins and need to be resuscitated, the tears of a mother, like mine, can move the heart of God. It is necessary that He speak, that He command through the priest in the Sacrament of Penance, and that the soul cooperate, then obediently lifting itself from the mud of its fault.

It is necessary, if you have the misfortune of being dead through sin, to come to me without delay, with these three dispositions: love, repentance, confidence. And then, I promise you to weep, to weep profoundly over the heart of Jesus and raise you to life.

And of Lazarus, what shall I say?

A stupendous miracle which astonished all of Jerusalem! Jesus was called by souls that loved Him and turned to Him, because He always turns to the tears and the pleas of those who are His friends.

"If you had been here, my brother would not have died," Martha told Him, and that is certain. When Jesus is in a soul, that soul cannot die. "Your brother will rise," He answered. "I am the Resurrection and the Life; he who believes in Me, even though he dies, will live; and all who live and believe in Me, shall never die." That is to say, he who has faith, will rise; and he who lives the life of grace, can never die.

And Jesus wept and groaned, because He so

loved those souls who were hospitable and loving. That delight of my soul wept because even such a great miracle would leave many hearts dead, now and in future centuries.

He wept! Oh, what tears of love fell down the cheeks of Jesus! He commanded them to take away the stone; and, lifting His eyes to heaven and giving thanks to His Father, He cried with a loud voice, "Lazarus, come forth!" And Lazarus came out, risen, although wrapped in linens. And Jesus continued, "Release him and let him go."

This resurrection of obstinate sinners, infected with vices, requires the tears of Jesus before the heavenly Father. It is necessary that He cry in a loud voice to His Father, imploring pardon and then freeing them from great obstacles and ties, with confession, repentance and penance, in order to avoid the occasions of sin.

I looked upon these miracles thinking of my future children, and you, child of my life, turning over in my mind the foregoing reflections: and now I do so for your good.

This is today's **Rose**, which I offer you. My **Thorn** was then to consider that my Jesus would not rise to stay at my side, but would at once leave me in this exile without Him. My **Thorn** was to foresee the innumerable souls who would neither rise and turn to Jesus to be resurrected, nor to me, pleading with my tears; nor to the souls who love Jesus and who have power over His loving heart.

My child, guard these reflections in the depths of your soul and meditate on them. Ask for my tears, dry those of Jesus, and be His faithful friend. Have faith, have faith, and do not doubt that you will see "the grace of God" here in exile, and in heaven.

RESPONSE

Today's lesson is beautiful, Mother of my soul! Which hearts can hold so much tenderness, love, and holiness as that of Jesus and yours? He cannot see tears without compassion, but He can shed them, yes, and ask for pardon for sinners and the life of grace for those dead souls who have offended Him.

You, Mother, who also dry the tears of your children, you desire to weep for me, desire that I pray for your tears, the weeping of my mother to whom God can deny nothing.

I am so selfish, my Mother, that I am even incapable of worrying about my brothers and sisters, of sacrificing myself for them and of crying for their souls.

What a shame, holy Virgin! How distant I am from resembling my blessed models, the heart of Jesus and your heart! Give me today the precious virtues of zeal for the glory of God which implies great sacrifices of abnegation and

77

self-conquest. It does not matter if I am weak and the cross frightens me: with your help, with your example, and above all with your love, I can suffer as much as is necessary for those brothers and sisters, immolating myself in whatever form necessary for the good of my neighbors and for the resurrection of sinners to grace.

Take my body, my soul, my heart and my life to be spent for so worthy a cause. Amen.

Today I will recite three Hail Marys for
the conversion of sinners, with my arms
stretched in the form of the cross, asking the
most holy Virgin to return many souls,
dead through sin, back to life.

MEDITATION XVII

The Eucharist

I WILL NEVER forget the first time Jesus confided in me about the secret of the Eucharist.

It was a calm and serene afternoon when I saw my Jesus, transformed and illuminated, as if a thousand brilliant suns shone within His transparent soul. His eyes were filled with tears and His breath was halting, His cheeks were burning, and His lips were burning as much as His heart. Overwhelmed and possessed by an immense love, I contemplated Him.

Then He drew near me, saying to me, "O My Mother! I am going to speak of a marvel which fills My heart with joy; a stupendous miracle conceived only by the love of the one God: the Eucharist.

"My love for man is so great that I sought a manner of being his food, his very substance and life, of giving this Body that you gave Me, this Blood which will wash away his crimes, of changing him into an angel, and of making divine life circulate throughout his being.

"Look how rapidly My heart beats at the very thought of a gift such as will cost Me My life—yes, the sacrifice of the cross which will be perpetuated on the altars. But this does not matter; My love for man is so incomparable that I shall descend to this ultimate extreme, even descending into his very heart.

"And this food for him will be so indispensable, that if he does not take it, he will not have life; and he who takes it, that is to say, who eats My Flesh and drinks My Blood, I will raise him up on the last day, and he will abide in Me and I in him; for I am the Bread of life and he who comes to Me will never hunger or thirst. Yes, I am the Bread come down from heaven.

"Mother, I shall institute this Sacrament of Love primarily for you because if I am not to leave My children orphans, I will not abandon you in your solitude, My Mother. I must be always living at your side, body, soul, and heart in the Eucharist. I love you so! … I owe you so much! … You were consecrated as My first altar and became My first priest at the Presentation; you will continue to be a victim with the Victim; and all will receive in Me, with your own blood, purity, the foundation of all the virtues."

And the day arrived on which, profoundly moved, He spoke to the world, revealing to those in Capernaum the secret of love which formed His delight. But—sorrowful disappointment! Jesus suffered the pain of being deserted by the multitude who said, "This doctrine is hard; … who can accept it?"

Then, wounded in the sensitivity of His love, He said to His disciples: "Do you also want to leave Me?" But St. Peter, consoling Him, replied: "Master, to whom shall we go? You have the words of eternal life."

On another afternoon He also came to me with immense bitterness and said to me, "I know that in the Sacrament of Love I shall be despised, hated, considered outrageous.… I shall bear these horrible profanations and sacrileges even from those whom I call My own.

"Nothing of this is unknown to Me, but I desire to be in the world so that you can receive Communion, My Mother, so that your devout ones will receive Me with love and because there will be many more adoring souls who will consume their lives at the foot of the altar.

"I will remain in order to be their Friend and the Balm that heals their wounds. A prisoner of Love, I shall seek companionship, ardor, consolation, for so many and such horrible sins.

"I shall place fire on the earth; I shall inebriate holy souls with the sweetness of the cross; I shall pardon those who offended Me and cry aloud to sorrowful humanity: 'Come to Me all you who labor and are burdened and I will give you rest!'"

And with the love of His heart overflowing, He rested on my lap. I dried His tears and offered Him shelter in those souls who would have the mission of sacrificing themselves for the Church and its priests:

- who would not leave Him alone in the tabernacle even at night...
- who would count their happiness in sacrifice, and delight in Him...
- who would move in an atmosphere of love and live from the consecrated Host...
- who, humble, simple, obedient and mortified, would give themselves up to pain in all its forms... because consolation for them is to not be consoled...
- who would be always pure and always victims.

What a **Rose**, my child, is this one which I give you, the **Rose** of a vocation as there is none more precious. Cherish it for its worth, descending from heaven especially for you; it has cost Jesus Blood and tears; it was earned by the price of my own heart.

Do not injure Jesus, my child, for the coldness of men, the ingratitude of souls and the solitude of the tabernacle still wound Him with bitter disappointment.

RESPONSE

Mother, Mother of my soul, Thank you! I wish I had a million hearts to express my gratitude.

Is a Eucharistic vocation—this priceless grace—for me, who merits nothing, who is unfaithful and miserable? Can I constantly adore Jesus in the Sacrament, I who until now have had only arrows to wound Him?

O **Rose** of my heart, which I am moved to kiss and caress! O Eucharist of my life, light of my existence, my white Bread descending from heaven through Mary! Come and drown me in the source of Your infinite love. How much I owe to You!

And how can I repay You? With a life of voluntary sacrifice, accepted with faith and love, without exhausting my faculty to suffer, rejoicing in each cross placed upon my senses and my soul.

Make me understand, Lord, how horrible an ingratitude it would be to betray Your infinite love; what a crime to answer You with tepidity.

This beautiful vocation is mine, in which the creature ought to disappear and lead a life through crucifixion with the Beloved, through adoration of the Beloved, through immolation in each Host for the Beloved, for priests, gaining graces for all the ministers of God.

A happy life, withering with the heat of the tabernacle, consoling the solitude of Mary, and recalling, one by one, her martyrdoms of absence. Yes, my Mother, I shall count your heartbeats of sorrow; listen to your confidences and weep with you, with those recollections of your Jesus and mine. Amen.

I will extend devotion to the Work of the
Tabernacles (the Blessed Sacrament),
and offer to Mary the cleansing of the
tabernacles of a poor Church.

MEDITATION XVIII

Immense Pain

M Y SOUL is still shaken by the recollection of how, on a Sabbath in Nazareth, the Jews wanted to hurl Jesus from a precipice, and passing among them, He disappeared.

Jesus read the prophecy in the Synagogue: "The Spirit of the Lord is upon Me because He has anointed Me to bring glad tidings to the poor. He has sent Me to proclaim liberty to captives, to give sight to the blind, to let the oppressed go free, and to proclaim a year of the mercy of God and a day of retribution." Rolling up the scroll, He sat down with majestic serenity and said, "Today, this scripture passage is fulfilled in your hearing."

And He went on to explain to them that He was the Messiah, the anointed of God, filled with the Holy Spirit, Who came to bring them the good news of the Gospel, to scatter the light of His doctrine of complete love, and to open the year of pardon.

And all who heard were enchanted. "All," says St. Luke, "praised Him and marveled at the words of grace which fell from His lips, and they said, 'Is this not the son of Joseph?'"

Then they commenced to murmur and envy; and Jesus, divining their thoughts, said to them, "No prophet is well received in his own land."

And, infuriated, they cast Him out, pushing Him out of the city, as far as the crest of the hill. They were going to throw Him from the rock when, with no more effort than His omnipotent will and with the command of His majestic glance, my Jesus made them open a passageway and, without haste, He passed through their midst. "And leaving the city of Nazareth," says the evangelist, "He made His residence in Capernaum."

What dreadful anguish pierced my heart on seeing that violent act of the Nazarenes who above all owed my dear Jesus only love, kindness, and service.

My soul desired to fly after Jesus and remove Him from that crowd of enemies who like rabid wolves hurled themselves upon the prey.

I ached in the depths of my heart at such ingratitude and because they were the cause for Jesus' leaving that village full of such beautiful memories, in order to go to evangelize other cities, less ungrateful, with the "good news."

My child, how terrible envy, pride, and grumbling are! Those vices hurt the heart of Jesus so that He abandons those who possess them. Flee from them, for woe to the soul from whom Jesus withdraws Himself! Do not be remiss in guarding purity of heart and innocence of soul. The beauty of love is so great! The beauty of humility is so beneficial! Faith is so lovely!

Never believe you know more than others; do not insult your neighbor; do not stain your tongue which frequently touches Jesus. My child, avoid the company of the wicked who are not beyond flinging you into the abyss of guilt, even to bringing you to perdition.

Always believe in the words of Jesus Who alone desires what is good for you; respect and submit to the dispositions of the Church and your superiors which He gives you, and you will be happy.

Look how Jesus abandons those who will not listen to Him. Read the holy scriptures every day because Jesus is there, living and breathing, opening His arms to receive you.

He came to cure wounds of the soul, and it is time that you run towards Him, your divine Physician, Who seeks to heal you. Remember that He said, "Come to Me all who labor and are burdened." Those who suffer, and you suffer, I know it well, my child; your soul is wounded in many ways, deep wounds which only Jesus cures. I wish that you not send Him far from you, because you expose yourself thus to His abandoning you like so many sinners, who mock His teaching and desire to put an end to Him, to His Church, to His ministers.

What foolishness! "The gates of hell shall not prevail against you," said Jesus, and they shall be shattered, they who maliciously desire such madness.

Today, however, before your eyes, as at that time, this prophecy is fulfilled, and the merciful Jesus summons the poor, those who are broken-hearted. And there are so many! He came to give sight to the blind who wish to receive it, and to liberate the oppressed.

It is the same Jesus, altogether loving and sweet. Approach Him, Who is goodness and gentleness personified. He is life. He came so that mankind would have life, and life in abundance. If He tests you, it is only to be richly rewarded: "If a grain of wheat does not die, it remains alone, but if it dies, it produces much fruit."

Approach Him and your sufferings will be relieved, because His yoke is sweet.

Now this is your **Rose**, in the counsel that your mother gives you in her solitude, and which she prays that you put into practice in the middle of your heart.

And my **Thorn**—what is it? At that time, the ingratitude of my own, in that village I so loved, the terrible impression of their hatred for Jesus, and today, that of seeing you, a soul that is hearing me, as I travel through the centuries even from the depths of my solitude, entangled in a multitude of vices which fight to thrust you into hell.

This has shaken my soul, which loves you so much. I hold out my arms to stop you, and my soul is moved to cry, "Stop, little child! flee—disappear!" and if it is necessary, change the city, the house, the companions of your life in order to be in heaven for all eternity, happy in the arms of Jesus and in my own arms.

Mother of my soul, I tremble at the very thought of being abandoned by Jesus. Many times I have deserved that He cast me from His heart. Pray for me, Mother; secure from Him my reformation and the reformation of my loved ones.

Do not let Him go away from me because I have wasted so many graces and I did not appreciate the gift of God. I confess my sin, I repent and I pray for His pardon through your intercession.

O Mother, carry my poor soul to Him, although I am unworthy of knowing and loving Him.

What would I do without Him, my Mother? What, without His companionship and His favors, His inspirations and His heart? I desire to form one spirit with Him, without ever losing sight of Him; one single soul, achieving likeness to that ideal of meekness, and of humility, hating my sins and my deliberate faults, all of which so sadden Him.

And when Satan, with his malicious deceptions, seeks to separate me from Him, stop me, my Mother, and offer the merits of the martyrdom of your solitude for my soul.

O Mary, help and Refuge of Sinners! Take pity on me and do not permit that I slip down the slope of vice and laxity. You are the beacon of my salvation, you are my Mother; and because of this my eyes seek you, my hope finds you, my lips call you, my heart prays to you, and all my being cries, "Mother! Mother!"

> Today I will promise never to gossip,
> but instead to be all loving
> towards my neighbors.

Seven Farewells

MY CHILD, shall I tell you of the farewells of my Jesus? Draw near, because I am alone, always alone, thinking of Jesus and you.

You see, the first farewell was terrible, when after the death of St. Joseph, my most chaste spouse, Jesus asked me to bless Him so that He could start His apostolic life. What a day of sorrow that was for my soul, which felt its life uprooted!

I blessed Him, sobbing, because I knew where He was going: to suffering and death for you, to preach and not to be understood, to teach a life of love and charity, and to harvest murmuring, calumnies, and even the sentence to an infamous death.

I knew He was going to labor fruitlessly,

because of the ingratitude of men, to sow **Roses** and reap **Thorns**, to cry to ungrateful humanity, "Come to Me," and to see Himself abandoned with the pearls of His gifts in His hands.

I remained alone with these memories of Him, but not as today, because I always followed Him from afar, serving Him and rejoicing to hear His heavenly lessons. All my pains I offered for you.

Another farewell, a sadder one, was that at the Cenacle; but that caused such a deep wound in His tender heart that, as He said to His disciples, "I will not leave you orphans," He also said to me, "You will not be left without a son," and instituted the Sacrament of the Eucharist.

Nevertheless, He was going to suffer and be torn, humiliated, bloodied. He was going to die, and I would not be able to embrace Him, serve Him, even give Him one drop of water in the burning thirst of His agony. He was going to the cross, and He embraced me against His pure heart for the last time.

O child of my soul! Do you know what it is to say farewell to a son who is going to die, and on a scaffold, being innocent, and only for His infinite love, paying the debts of sinful man?

In saying farewell, something is uprooted from our being, and so it was. O sorrow, which pierced my maternal heart! However, I offered this sorrow for you.

And my heart broke into a thousand pieces when on the cross, pointing to John, He said: "Behold your son." That exchange was terrible; as if everything was finished between us. It was harrowing for my maternal heart. Nevertheless, I accepted it, thinking that I would be able to do some good for you; that if you remained without Jesus on earth, there still survived a mother who is yours, a mother-virgin, a Virgin-Mother, who would teach you to be pure, to resemble the white lily sacrificed for your love.

You were already the child of a faithful mother, the most motherly who existed on earth; the most compassionate and merciful, upon acknowledging you as my child; a mother most tender to love—and this consoled me.

Another farewell took place when Jesus breathed His last breath, and He looked at me, as if to say to me: "Goodbye! I put you in charge; that soul is yours, save it, lead it to Me, because I do not desire that it perish; because I cannot suffer My heart to live eternally without it."

Do you hear this, my child? What does your soul experience upon hearing these confidences that your mother gives you today?

At that time I felt the sorrow of sorrows, deep, profound, bitter like all the seas. Everything had ended except my love which had grown to infinite proportions, and there was no limit to my bitterness and nameless desolation. Only the will of God, which I adored, stood between me and death.

I saw the good thief with holy envy, and had the desire to agonize and die. But no; no, my child, you remained; before my sight came interminable solitude, but it was necessary to merit graces for you. And here I am content, because I realize the designs of the Lord, His divine will. And again, I offered everything for you.

The next farewell was when the stone closed the holy sepulcher and one body and two hearts remained in it: that of Jesus and mine; or, only one, so great a unity had we known!

What terrible sorrow, comprehensible only to a mother! And I remained alone, alone; because everything was as nothing for me without Jesus.

Another farewell happened at the Resurrection. I saw Him, I was happy; my senses were reborn. By the brilliant rays of His divinity, my soul, my eyes and my heart, were illumined. I saw Him glorified, transparent, resplendent as a thousand suns, radiant with happiness and joy; but He left again. It is true that I saw Him again on other occasions, but He would soon disappear from the gaze of His sorrowful mother.

And at last, the most sorrowful departure for me was the one before the Ascension, because after He embraced me and I laid my head against His adorable heart, He loosened that sweetest knot, and ascended to heaven. "I will wait for you, My Mother," He said to me, and a cloud hid Him forever from my eyes, which shone only because He lighted them.

So here I am, in the martyrdom of solitude, waiting, hoping for the joyful day of my death. There, in His glory, Jesus waits for me. But my sons, the sinners? Can I abandon them, leave them lonely and forsaken? The joy, the crown, the consolation, and the happiness without end await me. He awaits me! But, O child of my sorrow, I had to sacrifice my incomparable delight for you, had to prefer martyrdom to joy, earth to heaven, only to teach you the fulfillment of the divine will, only to prove to you what your mother is.

RESPONSE

Your tenderness moves me even to the most intimate fibers of my heart. Thank you, my Mother of sorrows, martyr for my salvation! I want to be consumed with gratitude at your feet; I wish to make known those incomparable mercies of your most holy heart.

With what can I repay you for these martyrdoms of absence, which you suffered to win graces for me? With a life of purity and prayer, contemplating your sorrows, with a pure soul, crucified in your honor!

O Mother of my soul! I desire, at all costs, to be a saint, so as not to be separated from you for all eternity. Not at all! Never! But to avoid that, it is necessary, I know, to be your child, to imitate your virtues, to submit my natural inclinations, and to conquer myself through sacrifice and patience in my labors.

Mother, may I persevere in my prayer; may I be constant in my intentions; may I be strong in my pain. Please help me to always forgive my enemies, to return good for evil, and to obey without complaint.

Grant that I may know how fragile earth is, and how great heaven is; how short time is, how long eternity. Teach me, beloved Mother, to prepare for death, to bear my sorrows smilingly, to live by faith and to be a loyal companion in your solitude, in order to greet you in heaven and enjoy your company forever in eternity. Amen.

Today I will accompany Mary in her farewells, so greatly forgotten by her children, meditating frequently on her sorrows, and teaching them to other souls.

A Debt

*U*PON INSTITUTING the Sacrament of the Eucharist, Jesus said, "Do this in memory of Me." He was asking us to remember Him, only one memory of Him, because He knew that anyone who would think about His goodness could not sin. Jesus gave Himself to us, but at what a cost!

He instituted the Sacrament mainly to console my solitude, to stay by my side, hidden in the sacramental species, to give that unique food to my heart: His company. He did not want to be separated from me, for I was His inseparable companion. I was the Virgin-ewe, who followed the unstained Lamb in His weariness, in His worry and humiliation, even to His sacrifice on Calvary. I was, as St. Epiphanius says, "the perpetual companion of Jesus": fifteen years before His birth, thirty-three years during His most holy life, and twenty-four after His Ascension (because Jesus is at my side through His bloodless sacrifice), offering myself with Him to the eternal Father for the salvation of the world.

Moreover, in the Eucharist, Jesus seeks that you form a mystical body with Him, with the same blood, the same heartbeat and will, in order to be one with Him (as He is one with the

Father), in the unity of the Holy Spirit.

This intimate rapport and transformation is that which He seeks. For that He descended into the world and gave Himself in the Sacrament, in order to render payment to the eternal Father for the grace of the Eucharist, which He purchased in the Cenacle and which, with me, He began to pay for on Calvary. My child, Calvary was the price of the Eucharist; all my sorrows and my martyrdom of solitude, and all those of redeemed humanity, which are united to them, are still paying such a divine debt.

This is not excessive, my child, because its price is infinite. This is the reason why souls, principally victim-souls, and all Christians, must contemplate the Passion of Jesus—as a part they share in the humanity of Jesus—to settle this debt. Every grace is costly, and since the Eucharist continually renews itself, it is continually being paid for. It is certain that Jesus gives Himself to us, but it has cost Him to do that, and this is not understood either by the world or by so many souls.

Well, then, my child, if you love me, you ought to offer your sacrifices to pay the debt of the Eucharist in union with my sorrows, for if you rejoice in the presence of Jesus, it is not free of charge, but you have to contribute your mite of payment, in union with Jesus, Who is the treasure of heaven.

And until when will this debt remain unpaid? Until there is no one on earth for whom Jesus needs to sacrifice Himself and obtain graces. The souls that transform themselves into Jesus and are most like Him therefore have more of an obligation to be victims with the Victim, and to pay, in union with Him, not only the debt of the world, but also the divine debt, which hardly anyone acknowledges, and which exists always, for Jesus is always giving Himself.

My child, it is clear that He alone is sufficient to pay this, for He is God, but those who receive that benefit of the Eucharist—this is to say everybody, good and bad alike—have the obligation to also satisfy it with Him.

You see, my child, if I have said that the Eucharist is a debt besides being a gift, it is because one must distinguish one debt from the other, and this is a debt of gratitude that man in no way can pay, it is a debt of reciprocation of delicacy, of love, which any noble-hearted person will recognize.

When you receive gifts, do you not consider that there is an obligation to make a return or to be grateful? Thus, the Eucharist, the Gift of gifts, demands payment in love and sacrifice. Love always requires payment in love, and no one can truly love without sincere sacrifice.

Another grace consumed me with gratitude

(and this one was one of my **Thorns** of love): that Jesus Himself remained in the Eucharist with the delicacy of His love, so that compensation could be made to me, for the ingratitude of men toward me.

Yes, this memory of the tenderness of Jesus overwhelms me; and as I weep at His feet before the Sacrament, He gathers my hidden sorrows, because to Him alone do I show their intensity. But, O my child, understand this: I show Jesus my wounds, not in order to attract His punishment upon my children, but always to plead for mercy for them; I offer my martyrdom in exchange for your pardon and for an abundance of graces for your salvation.

This is a **Rose** for you, purchased by my **Thorns**. Do you desire to breathe its fragrance? Approach, and study the sorrowful and loving heart of your mother in this precious **Rose**. All my sorrows were for whatever touched Him, Who was my life, not for what touched me. I have never taken myself into consideration. I always hid under a veil of obscurity and forgetfulness, consecrating myself to Jesus in a life of complete humility, silence, and prudence.

Because, my child, although yet distant, the time will arrive when the Holy Spirit will lift up the veil of the martyrdom of my solitude, and make it evident to the world, so that, after many centuries, it may be honored.

Understand: if you seek to be exalted by God, humble yourself before all men: do not seek to shine; hide all human wonders and give the first fruits of your martyrdom to God.

Before I conclude, I am going to confide a secret to you: Jesus, in instituting the Mystery of Love, thought of me with more tenderness than ever, thanking me for having taken that Body from my body, and that Blood from my blood, which He gave to the world. That delicacy made me a martyr of love.

And another delicacy of His tenderness was this: that upon leaving the Eucharist to the world, He had the intention that priests should pronounce the words of the consecration as He did at the Last Supper—resembling me through their love and virtue (taking account of me from whom He came forth in His most holy humanity through the work of the Holy Spirit).

RESPONSE

O holy Mother of my life! I shall pass through the world hidden, obscure, opening my soul only to receive the warmth of the Eucharist and of your heart.

How is it that I, a poor creature, may hear the confidences and secrets of my Mother, when I am not worthy to lift up my eyes to look at her?

With what can I repay these delicate attentions of your maternal heart?

Although I am worth nothing, I wish to offer my slight sacrifices and sorrows in union with those of Jesus and of your own, to repay the beautiful debt which you have revealed to me and for which, beginning today, I offer the treasure chest of my acts of virtue which you will unlock at the hour of my death. I shall fill it with love and with sorrow, since only such coin will be able to help pay that debt, and I will unite all my acts to those of Jesus, according to His divine intention. O, if I were worthy to be received as a victim united to Him!

I know, my Jesus, that only You can pay and satisfy Yourself, God to God. But as a debt of love, of gratitude, of devotion, I am obliged to pay something also, and in this way to console Mary. I desire to have with you the likeness of a family, crucified through love.

If Jesus desires to be in debt, my Mother, I also desire it. O, what a sublimely great debt! To be in debt to God… to owe Him! Amen.

I will offer my Communion to the eternal
and beloved Father to pay for the priceless
benefit of the Eucharist, through the
very pure hands of Mary.

Triumph

I SHALL NEVER forget that on Palm Sunday Jesus left the house of Lazarus seated on a donkey, and as He was going down the road, a multitude came to Him bearing palms and branches, and putting their cloaks beneath His feet. They praised God, crying out: "Hosanna to the son of David. Blessed is He Who comes in the name of the Lord. Hosanna in the highest!"

A few days before they had been witnesses of Lazarus' resurrection, and the enthusiasm and the emotion of such a great miracle still endured. The triumph of that day was splendid! And as the multitude grew larger and larger, a hymn of praise formed by the clamor of sacred acclamation resounded like an overflowing river.

And when the Pharisees, indignant, told Jesus that He should reprimand His disciples, He replied: "In truth I say to you, that if they are silent, the very stones will cry out."

The entire city and thousands of strangers proclaimed Him the Messiah: the King comes, the Long-awaited One, He who was to come. Blessed is He! Hosanna! Peace to men! Glory to God!

And in all this, what did Jesus do? O my child, child of my soul! Jesus wept. His tears ran silently, and as they approached the city, He wept "with deep groans," says St. Luke. To Him, human triumphs were not important, for He saw the depths of hearts. He knew that the city would perish, that it had not recognized the day of its salvation; because of this, in punishment for its obstinacy, it would be leveled, and not one stone of its Temple would remain upon the other.

Jesus did not seek glory, nor vain acclamations which are as smoke. Thus, going to the Temple, He healed many sick, repressing the sorrow of His soul, since He knew that soon those same lips would angrily ask for his death.

And amidst it all, the voices of the children deafened the air with perfect praise. There was feverish enthusiasm.

But the hour to dine approached, and since no one had invited Jesus, He had no choice but to go with his disciples and retire to the open country.

But my child, will you let Him go hungry? Will you not invite Him, with all the sincerity of your love, to come into your heart? Is it possible that you would let Him go without detaining Him? I do not believe it; I know how much you love Him, and I cannot suppose, even for a moment, that you would permit Him to go away from your side.

O my child! Your **Rose** today is the lesson that Jesus gives you, teaching you about human ingratitude. Never be made vain by the triumphs of men; rather weep in the depths of your soul, considering the ugliness of earthly things, the envy of hearts. Open your eyes and see the payment of the world: its deceits, its egoism, its inconstancy which is nameless.

And my **Thorn**? What is it today, at the triumphal passage of Jesus? It is the fact that there are many men who do not know their day, that is to say, the day of the grace of God. They do not know that only one thing is necessary; that without Him they can do nothing, that they will be recognized as belonging to Jesus if they love one another.

And nonetheless, what do they do today? O my child, they hate, kill, seek after transitory and passing things which, like smoke, vanish with death. This grieves me, tortures my soul, here in my solitude. They seek the glory of the world, the triumph, the tinsel, the emptiness, the superficial and sinful; they do not think about death which soon brings them to eternal fire. How can I not shudder before so tremendous a disaster?

Flee, then, from all those who strive to exalt you, and, my child, humble yourself, hide, disappear, and suffer your sorrows in expiation for many souls of that time and of those who would come later, for those for whom Jesus wept.

Wipe His tears this very day, tears shed for love, and, on the corolla of my **Rose** of today, kiss those tears of my most holy son, Who wept in the midst of His triumph in Jerusalem; He wept because He wanted to show you how to detest all passing glory, all notice and acclamation that disappear.

Think about eternal life, fill yourself with virtues, merits for heaven. O, if you could open your eyes to reality, feeling the illusory nature of what shines, the inconstancy of the loves of earth. What could your mother give in order to convince you that every thing which is not God is nothing?

Meditate, think, stop and attend to this Mother of Good Counsel, who desires only that you be truly and eternally happy.

RESPONSE

My Mother, with what shall I pay you for your interest in my eternal salvation? Only with gratitude, carrying out your precious lessons in the actions of my life. Everything passes away except to have loved, to have known how to dry the tears of Jesus, and your own.

Jesus wept over Jerusalem—and that moves my heart to its depths. He wept for the inconstancy of the human heart which would change its love into hatred, its praises into demanding His death on the cross. He wept thinking of me, because I would betray Him so many times; because I would receive Communion in the morning, loving Him, and would give Him over to death in nights of dancing and entertainment which would destroy the innocence of my soul.

O false piety! I abhor you and resolve to take the way of the cross which is the only one which arrives at heaven; to practice the virtues although it costs so much; to make war on my vices, on my pride, on my vanity, and to live as I desire to die. My riches, Jesus, will be Your poverty; and my joy will be in works of mercy; I will see You in the poor, and I will feed them, remembering that blameworthy forgetfulness on the day of Your triumph in Jerusalem.

Each day You give me Your Body and Blood as food. Shall I not give You material help in the poor, and the virtues and the love in my soul to feed You? O, yes, Jesus, with all my soul!

And you, Mother, do not weep, do not afflict yourself, because I will follow your counsel and recognize the day of the Lord. Amen.

Today I will feed a poor person,
remembering the scorn which Jesus received.
I will ask Mary to obtain pardon for me.

The Passion

ND THE DAY that I so dreaded and that Jesus so desired arrived—Jesus, Who desired to give Himself and all His Blood for you.

I knew the terrible treachery of Judas. But since, at the hour of the Last Supper, in the moments of giving the world the greatest proof of His merciful love, the infinite love of Jesus concealed the one who was the traitor, I was also silent and pardoned the wicked heart which was to deliver Him up.

In a vision I contemplated the sweat of blood in the garden, and O child of my soul, I felt envy for the earth that received it. I saw Jesus fall from dizziness, covering the abyss open to devour you with His face, pale as a white lily. And I saw an angel presenting Him with a chalice, the same one that I was draining, without being able to give Him any comfort.

I saw Him hit and trampled on; I saw Him repay insults with marvelous love, led and dragged on stones and through thistles, until He received a cruel blow which resounded in my soul.

I felt the denial of St. Peter, and envisioned the horrible night that Jesus passed, spat upon and humiliated, suffering in the most delicate fibers of His loving heart. O my child! How cold and futile are all the words that might express my sorrows!

The sublime day of the Redemption dawned and I saw the sun come forth, trembling with pain, the sun which would hide itself in order not to shine upon this most horrible crime of the world. With a glance of my soul, I followed Jesus as He left the house of Herod, in the white robe of a fool, the people hissing and howling with furious delight. I saw Him as a criminal in the presence of Pilate; and the world shuddered before the unjust sentence of death.

I followed Him to the scourging, and, O child of my soul! I did not die only because I had to be your mother. O barbarous torment, which I will never forget!

O child of my sorrows! Let me take a breath in order to continue narrating to you those still vivid scenes which I still carry in my soul, and which I water day by day with the blood of my heart. I adored Him crowned with thorns, seeing Him the object of their mockery, when, staggering, He who sustains the universe appeared as a fool. What for? In order that a thousand worlds might fall down before Him, adoring Him? No, my child, only so that He should suffer the frightful humiliation which was given to cure your pride; to see Him presented as a criminal, and to hear the cruel and unjust sentence of death amid the frenzied applause of those whom He loved.

My soul whirled in that immeasurable space of blasphemies, of ingratitude, and of blood.

Then I saw Him bearing the cross, which He embraced and kissed with infinite love, like a companion longed for and desired, like the trophy of His victory. Its weight was enormous; I extended my arms to take it, and in my heart I longed to console Him, and as much as I could, to encounter Him at the turn of a corner, to approach Him looking at me, to kiss His face a thousand times with my spirit, His face which was imprinted on my soul long before it was imprinted on Veronica's veil—oh, yes, indelibly engraved! His adorable face!

And today I see it as living and breathing as then, with all the signs of his loving and sublime resignation.

I saw how He spoke to the women who wept for Him with so much love. And He fell and pitched forward, three times within my sight, without my being able to place my heart as pavement for Him.

And among the throng of people and the crosses and the thieves who accompanied the innocent Lamb, I saw Him mount the hill of Calvary, staggering, and I saw Him extend Himself upon the cross in order to be nailed to it, so that He might attract you to Him when He was raised on high.

Each hammer beat opened a deep wound · in my heart, and I shuddered from head to foot at the resounding of its echo in the hills; and when I saw that one hand was nailed, so that the other might reach the drill hole made previously, they fixed their foot upon the breast of Jesus and stretched it with even greater force, I do not know how I did not die. I experienced the dislocation of His sacred bones, and I heard, trembling, a groan from Jesus.

I saw how they nailed His purest hands, which knew only how to bless, and His sacred feet, which became fatigued in seeking you. Then I heard those last words of life, of pardon, of mercy.

Amidst the darkness, when the earth trembled and the trumpets of the Temple announced the evening sacrifice, I accepted as daughters and sons all mankind, and especially you.

During the three hours of torment I saw Him agonizing, and at the end, my child, dying without any support other than the cross, the nails, and the thorns.

The Blood of Jesus had been exhausted; the intensity of my torments knew no limits, when the cruel lance of the centurion pierced His side, piercing the heart whose beats were for all.

And I received Him in my arms and bathed Him with my tears; as the sun hid itself, I accompanied Him to the sepulcher adoring the cross, spattered with Blood; mute and shattered, I returned from Calvary over the trail of the Blood of my Jesus and His sacred footprints.

O, what a night! What days! And what sorrowful memories torture me today in my solitude, memories which would fill a thousand worlds if I related them. O, that **Rose** of the passion given to you today by your afflicted mother who so dearly loves you! How many are the **Thorns** in the Passion of my Jesus!

Kiss this sad flower, place it in your heart, and never part from it.

Each day, child, meditate for a few minutes on the Passion of Jesus, and I promise you that you will be holy.

RESPONSE

My sorrowful Mother, my solitary Virgin, I was your executioner, but it horrifies me to think about it, and I weep for my sins with my heart's blood. Give me a great love for the cross and let me die nailed to it, because I know, Mary, that you are immediately faithful at the hour of all crucifixions. A thousand times blessed is the one who dies at your side and whose eyes you close. From Jesus I learned to die; and from you, Mother, to endure death.

O Mary! I know that the weeping of your martyrdom gives life and I desire to weep much.

But first pull out this heart of stone in order that it may feel your torments, and pray for this poor child who greatly loves you, Mother, now and at the hour of my death. Amen.

Today I will accompany Mary
on the Way of the Cross during her return
from Calvary.

MEDITATION XXIII

Behold Your Son

ABSORBED AS IN a transport of profound sorrow, I stood beside the cross, motionless, going over the wounds of Jesus one by one, with my eyes and with my heart. As I was offering myself as a victim with Him, when, fixing His dying eyes on me, He said: "Behold your son," representing the entire human race in John, and pronouncing, in the depths of His soul, the name which I saw formed on His bloody lips: your name, child of my heart.

I bowed my head, accepting His adorable will, because those words opened new and inexhaustible fountains of love in my heart, so that I might be mother of all and of each individual; a faithful mother with increasing and immeasurable tenderness.

My child, I felt snatched away to a new

unknown world of sorrow; and I contemplated, as if under a veil, the never-ending number of sacrilegious and ungrateful men who would not love me as their mother, but who, steeped in the dew of the Blood of Jesus dead upon the scaffold for them, would run to throw themselves voluntarily into hell.

How can I not feel myself passing through many martyrdoms? But my sorrows were fruitful, because they were produced in my heart by a divine cause; they have a supernatural origin. They were therefore sorrows of salvation, because I united them to the redemptive sorrows of Jesus.

Unite the pains which you suffer to mine in conjunction with the infinite merits of Jesus, and they will produce copious fruits to glorify God.

Here in my solitude, I wish to confide a secret in you: when Jesus made me a mother at the foot of the cross, it was not only in order to engender children in my heart, children who would be born by virtue of His fruitful word. There on Calvary you were born. But perhaps you think that the mission of a mother, even the mother of mercies, ends when she gives birth?

No, my child. There on Calvary, I had hardly begun my maternal mission and I needed more and more years of immense martyrdom, of astonishing torments of love, so that, at this time, my heart would embrace the necessary and sufficient suffering which might buy each and every grace for all men until the end of time.

Consider how hidden and unknown for the world is this stage in which I purchased the title of "Mother of Humanity." The title of "Mother of Jesus" was a given grace, I repeat here to you, but this one of "your mother" was a conquered grace; the first one by the sorrows of my divine son, and later, can you not guess? … by my martyrdom of solitude. And this, my child, is not taken into consideration by my ungrateful children, century after century. A veil will always hide my virtues and my life, but when you read this, devotion to the Holy Spirit will be renewed and, as in a new Pentecost, shed a light upon your mother, His beloved spouse, in the martyrdom of her solitude; so that her glories shall be sung together with those of the same divine Spirit, since I was the instrument of His operations and of the extraordinary graces, the abundance of which were spread by Him throughout the world.

A powerful reaction awaits the world through these two means: that of the Holy Spirit and that of your mother who loves you so greatly.

The forgetfulness of these years in which the most cruel sorrows crushed me, and in which I obtained for my children, in union with the merits of Jesus, graces of all kinds for their happiness, will be erased.

And you, child who listens to me, will be chosen to give recognition to my sorrows and attract thousands of souls to my loving heart so that they may save themselves through them.

Receive, gratefully, in your **Rose**, these intimate confidences of your mother. But, do not guard them in your heart today, but allow other souls to breathe its pleasant fragrance and bring many of them to my arms, moved and grateful, in order to present them to Jesus.

Thus you may pay for those terrible **Thorns** which pierced my heart on Calvary, for the very sorrowful exchange of the Just for sinners.

I do not forget that I heard your name on the dying lips of Jesus; and here you have me, opening my arms, this broken heart, waiting for you, through the ages. And why? To give you a maternal kiss, my child; a kiss which you will always find in this **Rose**.

I am your Mother. You are my child.

O Mary, Mother of my heart! Oh, withdraw from me for I am a great sinner.

Do not ever place your pure lips on my soiled forehead because far from my behaving like a child, I have saddened your heart, my Mother.

But I am going to be good, truly holy

Virgin; I am going to be holy, pure, and a most loving child to my celestial queen, making her loved in her painful solitude.

Indeed, I will work with all my strength so that you will shine in souls with a new luster: the martyrdom of your solitude. But you bought these graces for everyone with the sorrows of absence because we are all your children, all born of your soul on that supreme day of redemption. Happy Good Friday! O happy fault, which won so great a Redeemer, which caused us to be given to so holy and loving a mother.

This spark will catch fire in the world, above all in souls which love you, Mary, because the Holy Spirit is, without doubt, He Who today lifts that mysterious veil which used to cover the most sorrowful period of your life. Many saints have announced this new impulse of your devotion, my Mother, a greater recognition of your virtues for these latter times. Will it be these, O Mary? Will it be the martyrdom of your solitude?

How happy I will be if I can use my life in being your true child and making you loved. Amen.

This very day I will offer to extend this forgotten devotion to the most holy Virgin, accompanying Mary in her martyrdom of solitude.

Tabor

TRANSFIGURED through the martyrdom of the cross, I received you as my child on Calvary. There, transfixed with a thousand torments and looking at Jesus with motherly tenderness, my heart said, "This is my well-beloved son." O, and how He finds Himself plunged in sorrow to save man! And Jesus, divining my thoughts as I contemplated Him transfigured as a victim, with Blood flowing from His entire Body, as from my entire soul—looking at me, Jesus said to John, and in him, to you, "Behold your mother."

This was my glory on Calvary as was the glory of Jesus on Tabor. The eternal Father pointed you out to His beloved Son; and Jesus gives you to me, to His beloved mother.

This title of Mother which Jesus gave me, do you not want it to be a **Rose** for you?

Will you not accept this **Rose**, pale in color, but sweet and fragrant, to gladden your life? The pains were all mine; but their precious fruit will be for you. Do you not feel this, my child, child of my heart? I am your mother, that is to say, the greatest possible being on earth. Happy shall you be if you are wise enough to understand this! How many changes would there be in your life if you were permeated with this very sweet gift with which Jesus has desired to honor you!

You fear, perhaps, that your ingratitude can minimize my tenderness? How little you know my heart, child. This love which pierced the depths of my being with a sword, this love which the words of Jesus created in my soul, is very deep and will always endure. From that time, I loved you as the apple of my eye, and I shelter you in the womb of my care, and I nourish you with my substance, transmitting my virtues, graces, divine gifts and resemblance to you; more than a beautiful mother gives her child beauty, and more than a queen mother brings forth kings.

O, if you could comprehend the immensity of my love! Study it, measure it if you can, and place this **Rose** of my heart upon your heart, for you are my child.

But I ask for your response, for the **Thorns** of your forgetting will be mine alone; of your abandoning Jesus, scorning the commandments, insulting the Church, and withdrawing from the Sacraments which purify and save.

That is what I lament in my solitude: the world of sin with which man, blind and ungrateful, will try to hide the mercies of God, annulling the Blood of the divine Lamb. How senseless!

You, my child, have offended Jesus, and not unintentionally, but with malice; not by chance but with intention; not in one thing but in many, innumerable times, child of my heart.

But today, at this moment, you repent and turn yourself to me, converted. The greater part of your life has been employed in thrusting darts into the heart of Jesus, my beloved Jesus; and I come to ask that you take them out of that divine heart with tears and contrition. All that, child of my soul, will bring copious tears to my eyes, but it cannot take from my heart the tenderness with which I love you.

Come, my child, do you not desire to make your tent beside the cross, as St. Peter said—near the cross of Jesus, which is the most beautiful spot for the repentant soul? Shake off your darkness this very day, and do not desire to be ungracious with your mother who has watched and wept so much for you; so that, transfigured by sorrow, she encounters you today to save you.

Please me by transforming yourself into Jesus through humility and through the charity with which He descended the mountain where He shone as white as snow, forbidding His disciples to report what their eyes beheld until after the resurrection. Thus you must "hide the secret of the King" which is not your right to reveal.

When, prostrate on the earth, on the Tabor of the cross, you feel frightened, you will hear a voice, the voice of your mother who, touching your heart, will say to you, "Arise and do not fear," as Jesus said to His disciples. You will travel by my side, from virtue to virtue, until you arrive at such a point where I can joyfully say, "This is my beloved child, in whom I am well pleased."

Mother, Mother of my soul, take this heart of granite from me, and give me another which will know how to be grateful for your favors. Is your Tabor a Calvary only because you love me? O Mary, my ingratitude shames me; my sins and negligence make me unworthy to call you Mother.

"This is my beloved child," you say to me, and I humble myself because months and years have passed without my having thought of your sorrows, without my remembering the solitude of my mother; but, heartbroken Virgin, I desire your tears more than all the delights of the world.

Love was your life, and your death a martyrdom of love because of the unrepentant souls which offended Jesus, the only center of all happiness. Your martyrdom is so sharp and sorrowful! Give it to me, pure Virgin; because I wish to share the pains of my mother; I wish to burn with zeal for souls, after I have purified my own; I wish to advance on the road of spiritual perfection, abhorring sin and its occasions, and teaching those who surround me that a saint is one who seeks—with a pure soul—no other joy than your love and no other treasure, after Jesus, than your heart. Amen.

I will receive a scapular, preferably that of her Sorrows, which has the privilege of increasing the love of holy purity in souls; and the promise of the holy Virgin, to those who wear it, to be present at the hour of their death.

MEDITATION XXV

The Thrust of the Spear

LOVE KILLED JESUS, my child, and hardly had He expired, when the rocks broke into pieces and the earth trembled. After such horrible blasphemies, nothing more was heard than sighs and sobs, breast-striking and clamoring for pardon.

Serenely I stood by the side of Jesus, to take His last breath, because it was for me. Life was over for Him, but love was not over, that love which even after death He wished to show you in the depths of His broken heart.

Only the Body of Jesus remained. His most pure soul had descended into limbo. My solitude, my terrifying solitude, increased gradually, and I did not die only because you remained, because I had to save you, I had to tell you something of my sorrows.

During this time what did I do? I offered my shattered heart to the eternal Father for the two thieves crucified beside Jesus. I was their mother, and it was time to save them. A little while later, one of them flew to the promised paradise. The other, rejecting my supplications, died blaspheming. Unhappy man. In those same moments as the redemption was being effected, that dagger was the most sorrowful my soul received.

But I lacked the ultimate and supreme act of martyrdom. The executioners, seeing that Jesus was dead, did not touch Him. Only one cruel lance, seized with devilish rage, shook above my head and was plunged into the divine side and broke His heart. What pierced the dead son pierced the living mother at the same time.

And the gate of heaven was opened wide— the window of paradise, the blessed abode of all the holy loves, the abyss of peace, of happiness, of mercy, of purity, of humility.

All of this and much more is the heart of my son, and there the soul will find a remedy for all its ills and security in all its temptations. This heart is the sun which burns the soul in heavenly fires. Who will not hurl himself into this fire, mounting the cross?

All the remaining Blood from that divine heart even wet my face and sprinkled the good thief, like a baptism.

O son of my heart! You can no longer experience the sorrow of this wound, but I—I felt that my heart was broken within my breast.

And Jesus, even during that horrible act of profanation, returned blessings for insults, because some drops of water from that heart fell upon Longinus and opened the eyes of his soul; he saw the light, and at once he wept for his sins, and confessed to the Savior of the world.

I have envied that iron which penetrated so deeply into the heart that my soul adored. That heart to which I had given its beating, and which throbbed no longer. That heart, the figure and symbol of the love itself, which alone knew how to love, to pity, and to pardon, was pierced by the cruelties without number of my children.

That heart, fountain and abyss of consolation, treasury of sweetness which attracted many souls to the cross, that heart which would lead to confidence, to duty, to sacrifice, was set there within my sight, dripping—because of man—the Blood which was left in it.

And I, as if petrified with sorrow, remained embracing the cross, sprinkled all over with the Blood of the Just One, altogether crushed in body and soul, without voice, without breath, without life; but firm and accepting the divine will with joy.

For me all consolation, all light, all happiness had ended. Hour after hour I remained adoring that heart which, later, nailed in the center of a cross, would come to remind men of the love of their God, and of the price which He had given for their ingratitude. It would come to demonstrate that, in order to reach it, they would have to mount the cross, sacrificing themselves.

There I stood to defend Him with a multitude of angels, who wept at the outrageous sacrileges; there looking at Him without tiring, I waited until that divine Body would pass from the cross on which He expired to the living cross from which He was born.

And thus it was that I received the holy Body of Jesus in my trembling arms; with all the delicacy of my love, I took the crown of thorns from His blessed brow; and, my soul burning with celestial tenderness, I tried to communicate again some warmth and life to the cold Body of my son, because not even in death did He wish to close His arms so that He could wait for you to throw yourself into them.

I kissed those hard nails and bathed His wounds with my tears, wounds at which sight my sorrows were intensified; and, praying to the divine Spirit for strength, I helped to take Him, the treasure of my soul, to the sepulcher wrapped in the shroud; and there, after reverently adoring Him, I again contemplated His face, a mirror where my soul was reflected, and covered it with the shroud. I had the grace to fix that final sword in my heart.

O my child! The flower of my soul has been cut down; love has broken it off. Take it, today, from my maternal heart. See how pale it is, and here and there, it is sprinkled with the Blood which fell upon it. Kiss it, child of my sorrow, caress it, clasp it to your heart; and, if you love me, bathe it with your tears of contrition.

This is your **Rose** of today. Contemplate whichever of my **Thorns** you prefer, upon its being offered to you.

RESPONSE

O Mother of my entire soul! Give me this **Rose**, Jesus, to refresh it with my tears of sorrow. It was I who caused His death with my sins; I, the cause of His crucifixion and His torments. Forgive me, my Mother.

Today I ask you for the martyrdom of love caused by the absence of your Beloved which you endured, the "I die because I do not die"; the soul, losing itself in unity, absorbed in the will of God, and only in God, that is to say, in the detachment from creatures, in the complete forgetfulness of the world and of all that is not Jesus.

Grant that my soul may be detached from the things of earth; grant that it may cease to be a lowly caterpillar and that it may be a butterfly, so that it may fly, even to be set on fire in the light of God, in the fire of the cross; and then, Mary, at your side, let me dissolve, die, reduced to ashes, crucifying all my desires and wishes for love.

I know that all this implies martyrdom, my Mother—but a martyrdom of love, one that is the finest type, one like yours, which I ask as your poor child. Tear out my heart today, turn its coldness to fire, and give me a heart that can understand your torments, that will burn and be consumed with gratitude, feeling as you felt.

Do not weep, Mother, because you are not alone, for there is one heart which will accompany you in your pain while living, and which will bring many loving souls to your feet so that they may plunge into the contemplation of your sorrows. Amen.

I will offer an act of penance in honor
of the solitude of most holy Mary, asking
that her love may pierce my heart.

His Heart

*M*Y CHILD, shall I tell you what His heart is like? Shall I reveal a secret to console you?

O, the heart of Jesus is a furnace of love, which loves and desires to be loved, whose delight consists in diffusing itself in souls of good will.

The heart of my son is the indispensable food for pure souls; it is that which enlarges and expands the channels of grace, spreading out all His treasures to the world.

This heart is a divine bonfire which invites you to sacrifice yourself on the altar; a delicious retreat into which you ought to withdraw; the spring of all good; the haven in which you rest on earth and your eternal happiness in glory.

It is the bottomless sea of meekness, of purity, of sorrow, of grace, of life.

It is the warmth of the Spirit and the light of hope.

What that is holy and sublime is not in the heart of Jesus? When would I finish telling you of it?

Well, I am going to tell you something as a favor for my beloved daughters, the women. I have testified that the heart of my son always gave them favors, according to the gospels, lifting them from the abyss in which they were placed from ancient times. Always, in His precious life of ministering, He permitted them to surround Him, to serve Him in His needs. They wept for me on His road to Calvary, and did not abandon Him even after His death.

He appeared first to them, and through the centuries He will highly favor them, up to the time in which, showing His heart to one of them, He will reveal to her His sorrow for not being loved.

The heart of Jesus holds the cross and the thorns. And what woman does not carry a cross very deeply, very profoundly in her soul? As soon as she is born, the world exclaims, "What a pity! It is a girl!" Growing up under the shadow of many sorrows, she makes her way through life, always with pain, contradictions, and struggles which represent the crown of thorns with which the heart of Jesus is surrounded, thorns of many kinds in all things, and this in whatever social class she belongs to. It is her lot to suffer; her patrimony is sorrow.

The wound of the lance! Alas, my child! Does there exist or will there ever exist one single woman who does not bear this wound in her heart? Disappointments, being orphaned, widowed, alone, stripped of illusions, martyred by jealousy, losing hope, and even being silenced in sorrow, obscurity, calumny and tears, she thus passes through the world, sprinkling it with the blood of her wounds and the water of her tears which many trample on and only God gathers up.

These flames which burst from the heart of Jesus signify His love. And who better than a woman synthesizes pure love, ardent and sacrificial? A love generous, constant, heroic and self-sacrificing; a love of abnegation without limit; a love of good will, of kindness, of consolation, because the part of this heart which burns has tenderness at its center, because that is its substance—love strong as death. Oh, yes! And for what is all of this? It is so because God created the heart of woman especially to love, and to suffer while loving.

The attractive light that shines from the divine heart can also be applied to the heart of a woman, because it has a natural, God-given attraction to lead souls to Him. If the ideal of the soul of a woman is Jesus, she can lead thousands of souls to Him.

A woman is the heart of the family, the center of the home, the focus from which the splendid light of religion radiates smoothly and easily. Society revolves around the woman and she can spread by her virtue, however she wishes, the essence of Jesus Christ.

But where is this center of the heart of the Christian woman? From where do these diverse attributes come? From my heart, my child, who am His Mother, the New Eve, the Universal Regenerator, the Mother modeled on the same Jesus so as to be His mirror.

Therefore, my child, allow me to speak: you must be innocent, modest, pure, and angelic. Your arms must invariably express all tenderness, all serenity.

You should be distinguished for charity, for prudence, and goodness.

You must be faithful, temperate, humble. You must shine in the eyes of God and of men for your simplicity, mercy, and sensitivity.

But above all, my child, you must temper yourself for suffering, for martyrdom, disposed generously to mount any Calvary without ever diminishing your faith, with increasing fervor, and always loving the cross in the form that the divine Will presents it to you.

And, more than anything else, you must love; you should receive Communion daily; you should lead an interior life of sacrifice in which you will acquire the strength necessary to struggle, to smilingly follow the road of **Thorns** which will conduct you to heaven.

Seek a good director whom you will obey, for obedience is the secure ship which takes you to the happy port of eternal joy.

Finally, since God has wished to favor you with a heart similar to that of my Jesus, do not dishonor it with your conduct; do not grieve Him with your inconstancy, but thank Him for the gifts which God gives your gender. Profit from them, for the sake of heaven, leading many souls there.

Take this **Rose**, sprinkled with blood, which is today the heart of my divine son. Kiss it many times, contemplate it enraptured, and fill your soul with its celestial fire. Raise it very high, even to the center of the cross and cry with all your strength to all persons everywhere: "If you desire to reach paradise, mount the cross; if you desire to hide yourself in this wound, sacrifice yourself; if you desire to learn to love, keep your soul pure by crucifying your evil inclinations, and renouncing yourself; if you desire to dwell there, die here first."

This is your **Rose**. And my **Thorn**—what will it be? If the hearts of my children have them, how many more **Thorns** will there be in the heart of the mother? If you see them, count them.

RESPONSE

Yes, Mother, I know these thorns and I wish to pluck them from your solitude, by putting today's lessons into practice. Mother, give me all the virtues which are necessary and permit me to be a living portrait of the divine heart.

What an honor! What happiness, what a holy motivation!

Cast at least one spark of your sacred fire into this icy heart, and mold me like the heart pierced by the steel of ingratitude, the heart which I love so much.

If you say, sweet Mary, that my heart resembles that of Jesus, what must yours be, Mother, martyred for love?

Then transform me into Him, identify me with Him, because I desire to throb with His heart's beating, weep with His tears at the neglect of men, to expiate the sins of the world with Him, and with your love, love much, and impress His sublime martyrdom upon my heart.

My heart is very poor, as you can see, but I shall unite myself closely to Jesus to offer it to the eternal Father as a victim. I will take this heart of the incarnate God—of an abandoned God—in my hands, and with all the strength of that heart, lose myself in the abyss of that holy love. There I shall die happy, because this loss is my salvation, and this death is my true life. Amen.

Today I will make a holy and contrite confession, to begin another life of purity and sacrifice, in union with Mary.

Solitude

I AM A MOTHER. Why would I not weep in my solitude without Jesus? "The same cause," says an author, "which makes mothers fruitful, makes them tender in love, and so strong is this sentiment that only God, who grants it, can comprehend it."

The cause of my fruitfulness was the Holy Spirit, Who is Love; and because of this I love Jesus as I love the same Holy Spirit, Love Eternal. My tenderness is a radiation of the coming forth of my fruitfulness. Can you even discern the immeasurable intensity of my love?

I am a mother. And of what a Child! Of the most perfect, holy, beautiful son—of the best Son.

I am a mother-virgin and the Virgin-Mother; so much more a mother, and so much more a virgin because I am the Mother of God!

I loved God in my son, and I loved my son in God. These two loves in one make my heart burst during my solitude on earth. Here is my body; but my soul followed Jesus in His ascension, and I can do no more than long for Him, with the most ardent and impetuous desires such as no human language can express.

There exists between Jesus and me a wonderful sympathy of complexion, character, temperament, customs, outlooks, desires, and will. Because of this, the same sword which pierced the son, also transfixed the mother, as Simeon prophesied; and there could exist no desire, suffering, or joy in the heart of Jesus which did not have its powerful reflection, its profound echo, in mine.

Yes, child of my soul. Do you now understand a small part of my martyrdom of absence without my Jesus, the terrible separation of two souls fused into one? Nothing is so sweet as the thought of Jesus, and at the same time, nothing is so cruel.

This memory is the fountain of my sorrow, and nevertheless, everything wearies me, chills me, and makes me suffer when my ears do not hear any reference to my Jesus, for whom I weep.

All the past, which renews my love, makes my sorrow increase. To remember His Passion is the most terrible, but at the same time, the most cherished of my thoughts.

I never lose sight of my divine son, not only because He is the most beloved object of my love, but also because He is to be imitated. I nourished my soul with His words and His actions, and constantly my heart was consumed with the sweetest fire from heaven.

In the Eucharist my soul bursts with the explosion of my tenderness; I retire to His side to long for His eternal possession, to weep with profound grief at the turning aside of sinners separated from the supreme good. My eyes do not leave the sanctuary, and they long for the beginning of my liberty after suffering for you; my heart will be unable to find peace while I live removed from my Beloved.

Upon Jesus' ascent into heaven, He took all my heart with Him; He took my soul with Him, and so great is the violence of attraction, the intensity and strength of our mutual love, that I can only pray for the strength to bear up under the sacrifice of absence. I console myself only with the thought that I stayed to give you an example of how to carry the cross, how to live on earth and reach heaven.

The tasks that you must accomplish are not to excite the admiration of the world. No, my child, you didn't come to shine but to hide yourself in obscurity and silence, imitating me. I want you to be holy, and sanctity consists in nothing other than subjecting your whole self to the divine pleasure, loving God much and suffering much for Him.

O, what science so sublime and precious as that of those who try only to please God, who are nothing in their own eyes, who pretend to nothing for their own sake nor aspire to anything other than to be ignored, scorned, shamed and treated as the most abject being in the world.

This I did: I humbled myself, loved and suffered much.

And what **Rose** do those interior sorrows carry for you? I applied the merit of my suffering to your conversion and through it sanctified you.

O, if you could comprehend the days and hours of sorrow which I spend in the desert of my soul thinking of you; if you could wipe away the torrents of tears with which I drench the pavement when prostrate on the ground, I purchase the graces of your vocation one by one, strength for your spirit, honey to sweeten your sorrows!

When I see you come to earth, I anticipate the beating of your loving heart together with mine, the zeal which you will display for the glory of Jesus. And immediately I redouble my sacrifices, cry to heaven, calling down treasures of blessings to surround and purify you, so as to form a **Rose** for you in my heart, which, refreshing your sight, will attract you to me in order to make you happy even at the cost of a thousand **Thorns** to pierce it. O child of my sorrows! That is love.

RESPONSE

Sweetest Virgin, delicate and holy flower, I venerate you in the sublime majesty of your sorrow. Make me love you, Mary; and then your pains will certainly find an echo deep in my soul.

May I feel your tears of solitude in my heart throughout my life since, through your martyrdom, sorrow sanctifies, and I desire to be sanctified.

If St. Paul the apostle prayed with ardor that the bonds of his body, which impeded his possession of God, might be broken, what would you say, Mother of Solitude? O holy Virgin, consumed in the volcano of divine flames, and alone, alone without the power to lose yourself in the ocean of light that attracted you! O Mother, who had to buy me heaven with your martyrdom! Thank you, Mother, thank you! Pierce my heart with the swords of your sorrow, so you will see, Mother of my soul, that I am full of gratitude.

I promise to follow your counsel, developing my desires of recollection, silence and prayer. Mother, obtain for me a great fidelity in small things and continual sacrifice of myself like lowly incense which perfumes the precious remembrance of your solitude. Blot out, I pray you, the good impressions that the world can have of me, and give me the cross, but a silent cross which will make no noise—a cross which bleeds in silence and obscurity, and which you and I alone may know; grant me, moreover, to live always humbled and scorned for your love. Amen.

As an offering to Mary, I will pass a day
of retreat, to savor her solitude.

My Communions

*T*HIS WAS MY CONSOLATION in my years of solitude, child of my soul: to receive communion, to receive Jesus in my heart, the same Jesus to Whom, as mother, I had given life in the Incarnation. And He returns it to me in Communion because only so do I have life.

Ever since Jesus ascended into heaven, the apostles have been consecrating the divine Bread: and I, generally through the hands of St. John, receive the Most Holy Sacrament. For me, the earth was a desert.

The solitude of my soul is sadder than death. I do not seek for comfort now, nor do I claim it. My only desire is to be able to console others, for as Jesus is my life, after Him, I am the life of the newborn Church, of the apostles, and of the disciples.

I am a Mother, and I must hide my tortures and dejection, the chalice of my martyrdom, before the tabernacle; and I must allow Jesus alone to sound the bottomless depth of my sorrow.

The very attention and solicitude of St. John arouse within my soul sorrowful memories of my lost Good. All the intensity of my pain flares up and all that I see revives thoughts of Jesus in Bethlehem, in Nazareth, in all places;

the memories inundate me with bitterness.

I saw the face of my Jesus, so delicate and pure, every day, every hour, every instant throughout entire years. I saw Him grow, develop, and change with the successive expressions of the different stages of His human life. I saw Him in the apparent naiveté of His infancy, in the enchantment of His youth, in the serene thoughtfulness of His manhood. I saw Him in the ecstasy of divine contemplation, in the indulgent tenderness of love, in the splendor of wisdom wholly celestial, in the sorrowful gravity of profound sadness, in the moments of grief, of disgrace, of heavenly agony; and each one of these phases was a revelation to me.

I could clasp my face to His with all the liberty of maternal love; I could contemplate those lips which would pronounce the sentences of all men; I could study Him as I wished, while he was asleep or awake until I had those pictures imprinted indelibly in my memory.

When He was hungry, His divine face sought me, and I wiped the tears on His infant cheeks. I washed His face with the water from the fountain, and the precious Blood came to make it rosy and more beautiful. Then I thought of the day on which I would have Him, pale and bloody, lifeless upon my lap.

I found ever-new delights in my Jesus; and with me the pure soul also takes pleasure in meditating on Him, studying Him in His different mysteries. When someone wearies himself in this, my child, it is because he is either not pure enough or not sufficiently loving.

His face was so beautiful (I will someday say to St. Brigit) that no one can look at it and not be consoled. Everyone felt a lightening of their sadness while they held their eyes fixed upon Him. So it is that the afflicted would say, "Let us go to the son of Mary," in order to feel a moment of relief, and rightly so.

My Jesus was so beautiful, so majestic was His divine brow, so pure and profound the expression in His eyes, so enchanting His smile, so sweet His voice, and all His bearing so simple, noble and divine, that He captivated all who knew Him.

O Jesus, son of my life! Where are you, Jesus? Now with every step I touch the terrible reality and water the soil with my ardent tears, hiding the formidable waves that drown me. I pass the days and nights in prayer, and I am the first adorer of the Eucharist. The few hours that I sleep are in continual contemplation, for while I give some small rest to my body, my soul continues penetrating the divine secrets of the eucharistic heart.

At every moment I fly to the tabernacle to talk with Jesus, praying for the world and sacrificing my body with penance for the sins of my other children. There in the light of the Eucharist I prepare the advice I give to the apostles. From there I draw the strength to encourage them, the fire to enflame them, and the graces to enrich them.

How sweet the night I spend with Jesus, fusing my soul with His. For this I am the model of adorers of the Blessed Sacrament.

But although living the contemplative life, I did not neglect my duty as mother, watching over the interests of the Church and the necessities of the first Christians, whom I served with special care, remembering in them my Jesus. I conversed with the apostles over the mysteries of faith and the life of my divine son. I consoled them at each step. I showed them that I was their mother.

And where do you believe that I lived during the years of my solitude? Except for the time when I accompanied St. John to Ephesus, I spent them near the Cenacle, on a piece of property belonging to St. Mark that he offered to Jesus and His disciples. Here, one step from where my Jesus instituted the Most Holy Sacrament; here, where the height dominates Calvary, where I have before my sight the terrifying place which was the theater of the drama of the world, of the most painful memory of my heart.

But I live with Him, for Him, and in Him. I prepare to receive Him, praying to the eternal Father for His tenderness and to the Holy Spirit for His fire, and inviting heaven to sing the hymn of love. Further, His real presence endures in my heart from one Communion to another.

The memory of Jesus and His words are also a constant Communion for me, and I offer Him humility for your pride, purity for your sensuality, fire and celestial ardor for your tepidity, and also the fragrant **Roses** which I give you for yourself. So receive Him when you read these lines which my tender heart leaves for you.

My **Rose** of today will be a tabernacle for your consolation; and the **Thorn** which makes me tremble, the sacrileges, child of my heart; those infamous outrages which my Eucharistic Jesus will receive in the coming centuries. Expiate them and receive Communion, my child, receive Communion with the most ardent love.

RESPONSE

Yes, Mother of my soul, I will receive Communion every day because however miserable and vile I am, Jesus is my life, and the one joy of my exile. The Eucharist steals my heart, and I promise to lead many souls as adorers to His feet, to console Him, to be His rest and His refreshment, His oasis in the desolate aridity of the present world.

Give us, Mother, your spirit of purity, of

abnegation, and of love. Give us your very heart in order to receive your Jesus, and allow us to displace the **Thorns** of your coronation with the **Roses** that your goodness has given us. May we always be constant adorers, day and night, in union with you, Mary.

Mother, give us that unalterable joy, intimate and profound in sorrow, which you know how to communicate to anyone who communes with your spirit. Give us the grace of never denying Jesus either a joy, or a glory, or the least consolation which we can furnish Him.

I shall happily breathe the fragrance of my flower today—Jesus in the sanctuary, born of you, Mary, and germinated before all ages from the root of all truth, beauty, and life—**Rose** of the Father and the Holy Spirit which I adore and admire, and which anoints all the **Thorns** of my exile with its virtue. Amen.

I will not pass a single day of my life without
a visit to the tabernacle in union with Mary.
I will receive Communion at her side,
always with increasing fervor.

Union with God

UNITY IS THE KEY to happiness; union is the object of love. The wounds of love are life-giving, producing unity.

What will the arrows of love be for my heart, my child, if not a union with the object of my tenderness? Divine love, unobstructed and to the highest degree, reigns in my heart. The intensity of this love is such that upon uniting me with my Beloved, I am transformed into Him, so that only by extraordinary effort do I continue living on the earth.

Even greater than unity is the transformation of my soul in Jesus—the soul of a poor creature transformed into divinity, so that day after day, hour after hour, the soul is simplified, enfused, and transformed into the supreme object of its love: God.

The Most Holy Trinity absorbs me, and in each divine Person I take delight, rejoicing in the infinite depths of their perfection.

I live so united to the Father, Whom I love with all the filial tenderness of which my heart is capable, and I so identify myself with His will, that nothing exists with which I can compare it. I praise His mercy, His fruitfulness, and His infinite power: I adore Him as Creator and recline my head on His most loving bosom, the beginning of all paternity, eternally beautiful, holy, and resplendent, from whence all things take life!

Through Him I was destined to be the mother of the savior, in order to crush the infernal serpent with my foot. How could I not melt with love for the love of Him? How could I not live united to His will and disposition? How could I not be an unresisting instrument in His divine hands?

And the divine Word? How could I not love Him? How could I not transform myself in His love since He took His most sacred humanity from my womb, since He lived with me in a union so intimate and filial? How could I not love Him, when because of Him I grew weak and withered, and I consume myself in this solitude remembering Him in all the years of His precious life until Calvary, until the Ascension, until heaven itself, with my heart, my soul, and my life being absorbed in the Eucharist?

And of the Holy Spirit—what shall I say to you? Ah, how I live in ecstasy with the intensity of His light, His fire, His sweetest songs of love. Since my birth He said: "How beautiful are your first steps, beautifully adorned daughter of the prince!" "Behold the beautiful house built for His dwelling by wisdom uncreated." Who inspired the prophets to name me "Virgin Land," "Incorruptible Mother," "Ladder of Jacob,"

"Burning Bush," "Tent, Fountain, Enclosed Garden"?

And when the angel said to me, "The Holy Spirit shall descend upon you and the power of the Most High shall overshadow you, because the Holy One to be born of you shall be called the Son of God," Who inspired him? And when a whispered warning led me to the mountain, Who inspired Elizabeth to salute me and made the Baptist feel the presence of Jesus? And when He was presented in the Temple, Who inspired Simeon and Anna, disclosing my secret?

All these memories confound me with gratitude. Even now, in my solitude, the Holy Spirit watches over me, supports me in my sadness, and I feel Him over me frequently, as at Pentecost, communicating strength in my sorrows and His gifts and fruits in measureless abundance.

All of which I have told you through these confidences of my motherly heart quiets me, attracts me, and unites me so profoundly with the Most Holy Trinity that it enables me to lose myself in that One in essence, in a single love with Him, and a single will: His will.

O, if souls would meditate on the abundance of grace that the divine Spirit sheds upon them each day, each minute! How intensely they would love Him!

O Holy Spirit, divine Fire, Love without end, Torrent of Sweet Delights, Union of the

Father and the Son! Consume our hearts, make them burn with love, and make them value the merits of sorrow that unites, purifies and saves.

One of the errors of humanity consists in multiplying interior and exterior acts, instead of unifying them in the Holy Spirit, instead of limiting them and having a oneness of will and desire with the will and desire of God in which true union is rooted. In the order of things, in the totality of exterior practices, which at times drain the spirit, many souls occupy themselves to their disadvantage.

It is more perfect to seek this oneness, to lead the heart and soul to this unity, seeking love and loving at the same time, through the Holy Spirit, with all power human and divine, to love God and neighbor with and in God.

Bring everything to this unity, my child; confide everything there, and with a firm look at whatever is divine, seek one single object, and focus all things in Him. How much souls would advance if they took this road, the shortest and the safest for sanctification, on which stands the cross with all its natural renunciation of self for the honor of God! Love is the incentive for all of those sacrifices; love, the incentive for all these martyrdoms.

In this **Rose**, my child, which I give you today, I have condensed the vision of perfection, the very highest perfection.

Love, love this unity by transforming yourself into the Beloved like your mother. This is what she did in her solitude. The souls that unite themselves most closely to Jesus through purity and sacrifice are those who obtain the most graces for heaven, both for themselves and for others.

It is necessary to simplify yourself in unity in order to unite yourself more closely to God. And how? By banishing worldly attachments from your heart, stripping your soul of all disorderly affections, refining virtues with the holy fire of the cross.

My **Thorn**, my child, is to see many of my children roam on other roads, erring on other paths, seeking the divine love without sacrifice, and seeing them die deceived by the brilliance of a false piety.

O, if such souls would do what I am now saying! How intensely they would live united with Jesus! And how even in this life they would be snatched very far away from sin, leading the life of the angels, with their desires and thoughts fixed on heaven.

They would feel the sweet necessity for atonement, zeal for the glory of God; they would live longing to avoid all that would sadden Him, and in that delicacy of a love which cleanses, purifies, and leads even to martyrdom, all because of love for Him.

Love, my child. Love as I am telling you to do, simplify yourself in the unity, and you will taste the ineffable sweetness of the true and indissoluble union.

O Mother of Mercy and goodness who always teaches me with tenderness the way to heaven! O incomparable Mother, remove the blindfold from my eyes and those of the many souls who travel, dragged away by the deception of what is not virtue. They have their hearts lost between God and the world, and they do not take the true road of the cross of duty, of love, which would conduct them to union with God.

Thank you for your advice and for your motherly counsel! Persuade me to give myself to the unity of God with all the strength of my being; so that, without letting go of the proper understanding of my nothingness and misery, I may feel my impotence for all good and may fly, grasped by the Holy Spirit and by your hand, without tarnishing my soul with sin and imperfections.

Grant that, instead of lifting my eyes to seek to understand that unity which would dazzle me, I may look into the depths of my heart, and there, though my eyes be dimmed by the brilliance of the divine Sun, I may look at Him, study Him, contemplate Him, and satiated with His infinite perfection, I will remain hungry for the divine. Is it true, my Virgin, that with humility, with purity of soul, with voluntary renunciation and such love for the divine will, I can reach union with God?

This is my greatest desire: to imitate you and have you smile on my poor heart, which is strengthened even to martyrdom for the sake of pleasing you. Amen.

Today I will try to seek neither my pleasure nor my human satisfaction in anything, in order to reach unity with God.

Adherence to the Will of God

THIS HAS BEEN the star of my existence, the end of all my aspirations, the passion deepest in my heart: the divine will, which I adore. There is nothing I consider a greater honor or a greater happiness than to execute it with perfection.

I love it so much that I prefer it above everything the more it crucifies me, because I know that true love of God consists in giving what costs us most, in paying homage peacefully to

His divine disposition, in submitting generously to those most terrible combats, and in uniting our will with His without murmuring.

It is willingly allowing oneself to be acted upon even though He may snatch from us and separate persons and things from us; it is throwing ourselves into His fatherly care and forgetting ourselves just to please Him. This is true love.

I love the divine will so intensely, my child, that upon receiving the message from the archangel at the Incarnation, it was the only thing I considered and I pronounced my *fiat*, without failing to recognize—in those divine plans—a life of suffering, a future on Calvary, a crowning experience of terrible solitude.

On many occasions I offered up my son in honor of the Father and consummated the sacrifice on the cross. My crucible on earth has been the adorable will which martyred me with His love. He asked me for the greatest of sacrifices, which I could not deny Him, because He, who infinitely loved His Son, offered Him in favor of the world. Reflecting this divine will, I also offered the beautiful little Lamb to be sacrificed in the temple.

The maternal love which burned in my heart and derived from the love of the Father, was almost infinite in my soul; this increased my sorrow in a manner which no words can express. But I did not hesitate for an instant, nor was

I unfaithful for even a moment; and with my soul shattered, I ran, always flying all the way to Calvary, to the sacrifice.

O, if you loved that divine will! How effectively would all your uneasiness be calmed, would all your sadness be dissipated, would all your confidence be quickened, and would all your love be increased! How your soul would increase in its brilliance—all your illusions would dissipate in it; all falseness, vanity, deception, and the nothingness of all that passes away—and you would be illuminated with rays of supernatural and divine light. Then you would find true peace, the intimate happiness of the saints.

Thus here you see me, my child, doing the will of God in this stage of my life, separated from that which I most love—my Jesus. Here I am, expecting the joyful instant of my flight to heaven; but I am conformed, resigned, content and at peace, desiring only what God desires.

I repeat often the words of Jesus in the garden: "Not My will but Thine be done;" the words of Jesus in Samaria: "My food is to do the will of Him Who sent Me;" and those others which astonished the listening multitude: "Whoever does the will of My Father, he is My brother and My sister and My mother."

I also remember with emotion, the innumerable occasions on which Jesus invoked His beloved Father with the most burning fervor, saying, "I always do the things that please Him." My child, waiting to end my life when it pleases Him, I repeat the last words which He said on earth and which still echo repeatedly in my heart: "Father, into Your hands I commend My spirit."

Love Him much, my child; only He is good, as Jesus said. He alone is holy, He alone the Most High. Consider that Jesus came into the world only to do the will of that beloved Father in Whom He lived, absorbed.

When He desired to implore mercy for you, He said on the cross, "Father, forgive them for they know not what they do." He taught you the Our Father, so that you would direct your gaze to heaven and would seek your consolation and support in that blessed and holy name.

Finally, my child, notice how Jesus pronounced the sacred name of His Father when He said that He had many mansions in heaven; how precisely He determined the true character of the adorers and predestined, when at the end, He said that only those who did the will of God would be saved.

Therefore, child of my soul, if you seek to be in my company in heaven, love, adore, bless and comply totally with the most lovable will of God.

This is my beautiful and fragrant **Rose** of today. Accept it, child; carve in yourself the likeness of your mother, always doing the divine will. If it is that adorable will that crucifies you, it is only to increase your merits and your crown in heaven. Oh, what ineffable charms the cross borne by love encompasses!

My **Thorn** will be your infidelities, seeing you flee from the will of God which martyrs you. But I do not expect this of you; I cannot believe it of your heart, which has received so many **Roses** from me. Is it true that you will never again pierce my soul?

RESPONSE

Thank you, thank you, Mother of my soul! I promise you, from this instant to throw myself into the most loving arms of this beloved Father Who gave me a mother in you, Who guards me as the apple of His eye, to Whom I owe every moment of my life. No, with the help of God, I shall never again pierce your soul by the **Thorns** of my infidelities, by fleeing the divine will, whatever it may be.

Certainly I have been ungrateful, and many times I have rejected those arms which you held out to me, for the world and for my own whims. O my Mother! Ask pardon for me, and tell Jesus that I will never draw apart from His teaching, from His commandments, from His tenderness, and from His heart; that I may imitate you by loving Him, accepting and kissing that will, even if it crucifies me.

He knows, infinitely better than I, the sorrows which will come to me, and although my flesh trembles, I want to despise these fears. Many times each day I will unite myself without reserve to the divine will in order to suffer whatever He desires.

All I ask you, my Mother, is to purify my soul so that, united intensely to God, He may snatch me like an eagle, far, far away from sin; so that I may live like the saints, like an angel in exile, always sighing to carry out the will of the heavenly Father. Amen.

Today I will frequently ask myself, "Where is my heart now?" Immediately, I will undoubtedly find the answer within me. And if it is not in God's will, I will direct it there immediately, with many acts of love.

MEDITATION XXXI

Longing for Heaven

*I*N THAT LONGING for heaven, for the Fatherland, for the Beloved of my soul, I live; that is to say, I die. Jesus is the center of my supreme attraction; He is the magnet that attracts me, drawing me into the infinite abyss of His beauty, of His enchantments and of His glory. Thus I die of longing to possess heaven.

There will be many saints in this world who will long for the sight of God with vehement desire—God Who will diffuse Himself in us, and will be the light of our eyes.… God Who will have us contemplate the irresistible attraction of the depths of His love, of that delightful and sublime state in which we will be entranced eternally in Him, participating in His own joy.

St. Paul longed to lose himself in order to be one with Christ, "to be made free of the chains of the body so as not to be separated from His side."

The psalmist said, "As the deer yearns for the living fountains of water, so, O God, my soul longs for Thee. My soul thirsts for the living fountains of God. When will I arrive and present myself before the face of God?"

St. Augustine's longing to see God forced him to exclaim, "My Brightness, when shall I see You face to face? When will that day of rejoicing come on which I will enter into the admirable tabernacle and satisfy my desire? When shall I reach the waters of Your sweetness? O bright and beautiful day on which I will listen to the voice of rejoicing and will hear, 'Come to take part in the joy of your Lord, outside of which there is no joy!' Woe to me that my sojourn is prolonged!"

St. Bonaventure said that this longing is unendurable when its realization is delayed.

St. Basil will call his longing to see God "an intolerable spur of desire." St. Teresa, St. Chrysostom and many others will weep with hunger for the vision of God.

Therefore, if this is the experience of the saints, what will I feel, the Queen of all Saints? If the children speak this way, what will the mother say?

O, my child who listens to these intimate confidences! For my heart, the time of my solitude is a most cruel martyrdom in which I find myself submerged. I long, hour by hour, minute by minute, to fly to His shelter—the shelter of Him Whom I love so much, to be surrounded by the eternal Truth, the cause of my faith; the Goodness and the Power, the cause of my hope; the infinite kindness, the object of my love—of the ecstasy of love, of that fathomless high sea of infinite love.

I feel that most powerful magnet which attracts me to heaven, and at the same time, the immense weight of my duties as mother, which detains me upon earth.

That's exactly why, my child, they call the pain of purgatory that of not seeing God, for there can exist no loss greater than that which deprives one of the glorious and perfect possession of the eternal Good; and on earth, there is no kind of torment to compare with it. I, my child, have no rest outside of God.

And how slowly do the hours pass for my loving heart! How long, my Jesus, how long? Night and day I repeat this, prostrate before the tabernacle, watering the ground with my ardent tears. It is certain that Jesus visits me, caresses me, consoles me; but He leaves me and this again increases my longing for heaven, and redoubles my martyrdom of absence which, slaying me, leaves me with life.

O what a lonely solitude! O life in which there is no life! O son of my soul! O loneliness which consumes me! O Love, my Love! When shall I leave myself entirely, leaving earth for Your embrace?

But what is your **Rose** of today? What is my **Thorn**, my child? My **Thorn** is to see that your love is so languid, that it is very far from experiencing the ardent desire for heaven, that your heart is too much attached to creature comforts that pass; their dust blinds you, hindering your longing to see God; their noise deafens your ears, and you fail to hear the melodies of glory.

The divine life is in you, circulating in your veins, and you do not know or value it. What can I do so that you will be in love with Jesus? What, to draw you out of tepidity? Think that He is the light of your eyes, the perfume that embalms your life, and the delight which will never deceive your heart. Why such great coldness for One Who can want only your happiness?

May it no longer be thus! And the following counsel will be your **Rose** for today:

Live with purity of heart, detach it from earth, and think that you are a pilgrim on a journey to her fatherland.

See death before you, the beginning of your liberty, and do not hold it in horror. Why fear death if it is a reward for those who are mine, a bond which is untied in order that you may become absorbed in God?

Love God, love Him much, doing His will, and you will lose the fear of death. If you fear for those whom you leave on earth, you can do much more good for them there, because union with God and His possession does not impede charity, but rather enkindles it by purifying and increasing paternal love, filial love, etc., for souls with whom you had holy bonds on earth.

In God you see all things and their necessities and remedies with the gigantic love that exists in heaven. Through a clear understanding of the divine, souls glorified in God tend to help others to give Him glory.

The affections of glorified souls do not die there, are hence refined and made divine, for the good of those whom they love.

O my child! You do not comprehend infinite love. Only God understands God, in the eternal abyss of His perfection and of His love. The Mystical Body of the Church is not broken; it is not dismembered by death; but in heaven, it continues its perfection, forming the Church triumphant that crowns Jesus.

Neither are kinships cut off; there in heaven where everything is happiness, their desires are satisfied because they are all pure in the sight of God, Who forms the complete joy of souls. All is love, all is holiness in the Holy of Holies.

RESPONSE

Yes, Mother of my soul, who arouses my faith, refines my hope, and gives me life with love. In Jesus, I find a dream beyond all possible dreams: all that I can love; all that is true, pure; all that is holy and beautiful; all that can charm; all that is to consume my soul, inspire a holy life, and the longing for heaven.

Having kept the commandments, is it true that I ought not to fear? Having practiced the evangelical counsels, I will be closer to Jesus, and, conducting myself as your true child, I shall long also to see myself free from this mortal flesh so as to fly to that place of perpetual joy and draw from the inexhaustible spring, which is God.

There I shall enjoy all the benefits, and not simply one at a time. United to the infinite Intelligence, I shall see all beloved beings in one infinite Being; moreover, I shall be the possessor of the whole God.

I will also contemplate you, Mary, and just knowing you would make all martyrdoms seem as nothing. Give me, Mother, now that you are engulfed in the divinity, some gleam of your light, that will make me somehow see the perfect love of heaven which is finally to be enjoyed.

I will forget myself, scorning all that
passes and tarnishes; I will desire only
the glory of God, through Mary, at the cost
of whatever sacrifice. My feet shall be upon
earth, but my soul, my conversations,
and all my heart will be in heaven,
seeking Jesus and Mary.

MEDITATION XXXII

Mary Died!

ATHER NIEREMBERG writes that an angel announced to me that my death was drawing near. Full of heavenly joy, I advised St. John, and this beloved son told his companions, the other apostles who (except St. Thomas, who arrived after my death), were miraculously gathered on Mount Zion and surrounded me, full of sorrow.

There, consumed with celestial nostalgia, and burning with ecstatic ardor, my soul breathed forth these passionate lines of the Song of Songs: "I exhort you, O daughters of Jerusalem, if you find my Beloved, to tell Him that I faint with love, love strong as death, jealousy hard as hell: its coals, burning coals and a torrent of flames;... comfort me with flowers, refresh me with apples, for I faint with love."

One happy day I finally heard the voice of the Beloved saying to me, "Arise, make haste, My love, My dove, My beautiful one, and come."

O, child of my soul, that "come" resounded in my heart like the most delightful music of heaven! There at last I would see Jesus, throw myself into His divine embrace, live at His side, and never be separated from Him. For me, the crowns that awaited me were nothing, provided that I live in His company and give you my favors in great abundance.

After the Ascension of my divine son, I was more humble than ever, more than ever the "handmaid of the Lord," and of mankind, until I vanished into oblivion and humility. But the more one humbles himself, the more God exalts him; and then, as never before, He Who is all-powerful did great things for me, surprising even heaven itself which said, "Who is this that comes forth as the dawn, fair as the moon, bright as the sun?" But why all this, my child? Because

I lived after Jesus with the greatest resignation, with absolute patience, suffering the incredible martyrdom of absence. My fidelity was incomparable in that long exile where I had purchased graces for you.

Later, St. Bernard would say, "The Ascension of the Son and the Assumption of the mother were necessary to scatter an abundance of graces over the earth. Jesus had to return to the Father in order to send His Holy Spirit to the apostles, and Mary had to return to her son to communicate His merits to men."

My jubilation had no equal. I blessed the apostles and disciples of Jesus, the newborn Church and all future Christians among whom you can count yourself. I expired sweetly in the power of divine love, and lifted in the arms of the angels, leaning upon the breast of my Jesus, I was carried to the celestial mansions, to occupy the throne prepared above all choirs of angels, and crowned by the Blessed Trinity.

But one **Thorn** pierced my soul, my child, and that was to be separated from you; to abandon you alone in this exile, to be removed from your side, to leave you in this valley of tears. But later that grief turned into the joy of heaven when I felt the power of the title, "Queen of All Saints" to make you holy; "Health of the Sick" to cure your ills; "Refuge of Sinners" to shelter you in my heart; "Virgin Most Faithful" never to abandon you. This is the heart of your Mother. Contemplate and admire it.

And so here you have me, child of my soul, showing Jesus every day the **Roses** and **Thorns** which crown my heart for your good. I often show Him that **Rose** of love, of mercy, that says "Mother"; and His kindness denies me nothing; rather He has placed in my hands all graces and virtues, all roses and gardens, with which to sweeten your life, and palms and crowns to reward you.

Already the winter is passed for me, and it will pass for you. I await for you here; come, come; endure and suffer today so as to rejoice tomorrow. "Come from Lebanon, my spouse, come from Lebanon; come and be crowned." I desire that your ears hear, on the day of your death, that very sweet "Come," and that you will be crowned with the crown of graces, for on earth you loved me, accompanying me in my sad hours of solitude.

But before I leave you, I am going to give you some reflections:

Perhaps, my child, you are made happy by the glory of this world, its riches, pleasures, and power? No, child, no; you are made happy by poverty, obedience, humility, suffering, obscurity, endless crosses, if you accept and use all of these things with faith and love. Lock your heart against selfishness. Be all to all, because outside that divine atmosphere, which infinite love and the cross formed for you, there will exist for you neither light nor life nor certainty nor peace nor joy nor heaven if you do not breathe the virtues and practice them.

Look, child, one more point for your relief. Souls who meditate on my sorrows are not lost, for I will love them and I will attain graces for them. To my favored souls, heaven belongs: to those who cry with me in my solitude and extend devotion to me, I will fly to give counsel, above all at the hour of their death. Do not be afraid; do not allow your heart to be saddened because where I am, you can be—and very soon, if you are pure, if you love the cross, if Jesus is your life.

My blue mantle will always enfold you, and the heart of your mother, who has gifted you with all of her **Roses**, will watch over you.

Do not weep. I am going at last with my Jesus, but I will return at Lourdes, at Fatima, and at Tepeyac [the site where Our Lady of Guadalupe appeared] where I will leave my image for your consolation. Let nothing disturb your heart because I leave you the Eucharist. In this you will have the Blood which Jesus took from me.

You know where I am going, and on what road to follow me, the way of sorrow, of Calvary, of solitude on earth. "To know how to suffer, how to bear the cross, to die: this is the science of the saints."

Whoever loves me will love Jesus, keep His commandments, extend His glory, and practice the virtues, imitating me in my self-denial and in my love for God, the principal cause of my sorrows, when I see Him forgotten and offended.

Jesus has given some souls the grace of resembling Him with the external stigmata of His wounds, marks of the lash, etc., but to me was given His total interior resemblance, above all after His passion, with all that His heart suffered. In this you can imitate me, my child; it is a grace that your mother gives you as she goes to heaven. The image of Jesus will be imprinted on your soul, but it will be a sorrowful one, and you will taste my bitterness, not only accompanying me in my exterior solitude but moreover feeling in your heart the echo of my sorrows, the reflection of my tears, with the same end of redemption and glorification: the salvation of souls; the glory and triumph of the Church of God.

And do not believe that this manifestation—the manifestation of my martyrdom, of my solitude in the absence of Jesus—is going to be a sadness for humanity; no, my child. My sorrows will be celebrated as fruits of multiple graces and sweet delights for souls and this is the **Rose** for my children that hides the **Thorns**, the bitter sorrows of the mother. That which is seen in the **Roses** will remain—that is to say, the fruit conquered by my tears, but gratitude will quicken and there will come from the grave of forgetfulness as many martyrdoms as my children have crowns in heaven.

Now I conclude the gift of my confidences with the last **Rose** which, before dying, I removed from my motherly heart for you; and the **Thorns** of your mother will also end. Be glad, and drive them all into your heart in order to complete the passion of Jesus on earth.

I desire only to make you happy. And in what does happiness consist? In that transport of the soul which goes out of itself to enter into union with God.

RESPONSE

Yes, Mother of my life! I accept the gift of your heart with all my soul. I clasp the sorrowful image of Jesus in my arms, and I long to experience the suffering which you announce to me as necessary to be your companion. Thank you, my Mother! With your help, and with the love of Jesus in which I am consumed, I will be able to do all, even to reach heaven with my cross.

My love will lie in suffering, will triumph in humility, imitating you, identifying my will and intentions and my entire life with Jesus, having only one life in Him. I will be happy, my Mother, if I suffer continually in body and soul, sure that such a state will be one of your most precious blessings to detach me from earth and unite me to God.

One thought saddens me. What shall I do on earth, my Mother, without the daily **Rose** of my loving mother which exhales the aroma of her heart? I shall again go over these confidences every day of my life, to inebriate myself with the perfume of Calvary. It is a joy for me to contemplate you engulfed in immense happiness, illumined with eternal light, but not forgetting your poor children. Oh, yes! Remember me, my Mother; see my tears, my terrible loneliness, my hidden suffering, and bless me always, always without removing your gaze from one who can do nothing without you.

Farewell, Mother of my soul. Be happy and do not delay in coming for me. Amen.

I will rule out of myself today my desire for
human praise, which is as smoke, and
fear of punishment so as not to excuse myself; in the tedium of setbacks,
I will smile; in the discomfort of antipathy
I will be loving. Moreover, I will keep an
evenness of temper, always humble, amiable,
self-sacrificing, storing up graces for heaven.
And all for Mary, all in union with Mary,
praying for a happy death.

The Assumption

MARY WENT to the grave as her divine son did, to be like Him in everything. Having been preserved from original sin, and from all faults, she did not know the corruption of the sepulcher. Her resurrection was immediate.

A tradition recounts that, having reached the age of 72 years (in the year 57 or 58), the holy Virgin reunited around her bed the disciples, who, having dispersed, were evangelizing the nations; and that then accompanied by a celestial melody, they were shown a vision of angels, who lifted the stainless soul of Mary to the bosom of God.

Meanwhile her body was carried by the apostles in the midst of a choir of angels, because she was the queen of both, and was placed in a sepulcher near the Garden of Gethsemane. Three days later, when St. Thomas arrived and wanted to see and honor that temple of God for the last time, the sepulcher was opened, and the body of Mary was no longer in it.

They could find only the linens in which she had been wrapped and which gave off a celestial fragrance. Overwhelmed with admiration, and assisted by the Holy Spirit, they interpreted that He who had deigned to become incarnate in the womb of Mary, ever Virgin, determined to transport her uncorrupted and immaculate body to glory, animating it anew, without awaiting the general resurrection. Joining the apostles was the first bishop of Ephesus, Timothy, and Dionysius, the Areopagite (says St. John Damascene).

"If upon inviting those chosen ones into His Kingdom, Jesus would say to them, "Come, blessed of My Father…," surely He said to Mary, as suggested by a pious disciple of St. Bernard, "Come, O My beloved! As nobody gave Me more in the world, so I desire none to be given more in glory.

"At the Incarnation, you gave Me that which is natural to men. At the assumption, I desire to give you that which is the grandeur of God.

"You enclosed a God-child in your womb, and you will receive the immense God in His glory.

"You gave a place of repose to God on His journey; and you will be a palace of God reigning in His kingdom.

"You gave a place to God the militant, and you will be the triumphant chariot of God the victor. You were a place of repose to the Incarnate Spouse, and here you will be the throne of the crowned King."

O admirable welcoming of God, Who knew so well how to repay the love and sacrifices of Mary! The glory corresponds with the grace; and if the angel saluted her at the incarnation "full of grace," what can the multiplied degree of sanctity be, increased at each instant from height to height, attained by her at her death? "Her soul was of such sanctity," says one author, "that it lifted her body to the level of the celestial region."

Mary ascended to the most elevated throne in heaven to receive the reward of highest virtue, with a glory proportioned to her love, her humility, her sorrows. The Blessed Trinity came out to crown her with a triple crown of Daughter, Spouse, and Mother. St. Joseph, her loving spouse on earth, and each choir of angels brought her new scepters, and the prophets, with all heaven full of jubilation, proclaimed her their queen.

On contemplating the queen, Moses joyfully would repeat, "Out of Jacob will arise a new star, and the staff of Israel shall bud forth."

Assisted by the Spirit of God, Isaiah would repeat, "This is the Virgin who shall conceive and bring forth a Son."

Ezekiel would recognize the sealed door through which no one should ever enter, except the God of Hosts.

David would repeat those psalms which he used to chant so enthusiastically, "The main glory of the King's daughter is within." "Listen, O daughter, and consider. Incline your ear and forget your people and your father's house, and the King shall desire you in your beauty." "The Most High has sanctified His tabernacle." "At Your right hand is the Queen with vestments embroidered in gold and variously adorned."

And Solomon would add, "Balsam scattered is your name, O most beautiful among women!" "Oh, how beautiful you are, My beloved! How fair, with your eyes like those of a dove!" "I am the flower of the field and the lily of the valley." "Like a lily among thorns, so is My beloved among the maidens."

And in gestures of love, the whole court of heaven would salute her joyfully. Arriving at last in the center of their sovereign charms with modest astonishment, finding all heaven beneath her feet, Mary would break into that sublime canticle, repeating, "My soul magnifies the Lord... because He has looked graciously on the lowliness of His handmaid, for behold, from henceforth all generations shall call me blessed."

RESPONSE

Mother of my soul, Virgin Mary; you went to rejoice eternally among the rewards and crowns, the divine compliments of your beloved, bought with your sorrows. But I know that you will not forget me; that in your motherly heart echo smothered cries for the sorrows of your poor children. I know that you love me much, so much; and that, loving and compassionate, you look down at me from your throne, whose pedestal the cherubim and seraphim form. I know what you are for me, Mary, and here hold the crown of **Roses** of your martyrdom that I pray you will place on my brow at the hour of my death.

For your incomparable glory, but even more for your sorrows and **Thorns**, I pray that, at the hour of my passing from this world to the other, you may be present, very close to me, and that one of your tears will fall upon the balance of my destiny so as to obtain eternal happiness.

Remember, Mother, that I am your child; that although I do not merit it, you are my Mother; and that in this exile where I still wander, I weep with you, O Mother—Mother of my soul! I sympathize with your martyrdom of solitude. Amen.

ST PAULS

This book was produced by ST PAULS/Alba
House, the Society of St. Paul, an international
religious congregation of priests and brothers
dedicated to serving the Church through the
communications media.

For information regarding this and associated
ministries of the Pauline Family of Congre-
gations, write to the Vocation Director, Society
of St. Paul, 2187 Victory Blvd., Staten Island,
New York 10314-6603. Phone (718) 982-5709;
or E-mail: vocation@stpauls.us or check our
internet site, www.vocationoffice.org